THE MURDER OF
EMMETT TILL

THE MURDER OF EMMETT TILL

KARLOS K. HILL

DAVID DODSON

New York   Oxford
OXFORD UNIVERSITY PRESS

Oxford University Press is a department of the University of Oxford.
It furthers the University's objective of excellence in research, scholarship,
and education by publishing worldwide. Oxford is a registered trade mark of
Oxford University Press in the UK and certain other countries.

Published in the United States of America by Oxford University Press
198 Madison Avenue, New York, NY 10016, United States of America.

For titles covered by Section 112 of the US Higher Education
Opportunity Act, please visit www.oup.com/us/he for the latest
information about pricing and alternate formats.

Library of Congress Cataloging-in-Publication Data
Names: Hill, Karlos K., author. | Dodson, David, 1966- illustrator.
Title: The murder of Emmett Till / Karlos K. Hill, David Dodson.
Description: New York, NY : Oxford University Press, [2021] | Series:
   Graphic history series | Summary: "The Murder of Emmett Till's primary
   aim is to commemorate the 1955 Emmett Till murder by providing an
   up-to-date and concise narrative of the murder that is reflective of the
   latest scholarship and recent developments in the case such as the
   Federal Bureau of Investigation's (FBI) reopening of the Emmett Till
   murder case in 2004, the US Senate's formal apology for lynching in
   2005, the FBI's 2006 Emmett Till murder investigative report, and the
   passage of the 2008 Emmett Till Unsolved Crimes Act"— Provided by
   publisher.
Identifiers: LCCN 2019059743 (print) | LCCN 2019059744 (ebook) | ISBN
   9780190216016 (paperback) | ISBN 9780190926250 (epub) | ISBN
   9780190084967 (ebook)
Subjects: LCSH: Till, Emmett, 1941-1955. |
   Lynching—Mississippi—History—20th century. | African
   Americans—Crimes against—Mississippi. |
   Racism—Mississippi—History—20th century | Till, Emmett,
   1941-1955—Comic books, strips, etc. |
   Lynching—Mississippi—History—20th century—Comic books, strips, etc.
   | African Americans—Crimes against—Mississippi—Comic books, strips,
   etc. | Racism—Mississippi—History—20th century—Comic books, strips,
   etc.
Classification: LCC HV6465.M7 H55 2021 (print) | LCC HV6465.M7 (ebook) |
   DDC 364.1/34 [B]—dc23
LC record available at https://lccn.loc.gov/2019059743
LC ebook record available at https://lccn.loc.gov/2019059744

Printing number: 9 8 7 6 5 4 3 2 1

Printed by LSC Communications, Inc.,
United States of America

For Mamie and all those who have sought justice for Emmett Till

CONTENTS

LIST OF MAPS

PREFACE

I am a historian of lynching and racial violence. My scholarship and teaching have revolved around understanding how black Americans have experienced, made sense of, and ultimately responded to white terrorist violence. Perhaps more than any other instance of racial violence, the story of how in 1955 a fourteen-year-old black youth named Emmett Till from Chicago traveled to Mississippi and was brutally murdered for whistling at a white woman has been foundational to my teaching and research. Beyond Till's importance to me as a scholar-teacher, as a father of twin six-year-olds, I relate to his story. Till's murder by white racists resonates with me and in many ways represents my deepest fears as a parent of black children because I am deeply cognizant of the persistence of white supremacist violence in contemporary American society.

Despite my personal and professional engagement with Till's story, I had never considered writing a book about it. That changed in December 2013 when Brian Wheel, then an Oxford University Press editor, encouraged me to think about a potential book we could collaborate on. After a brief conversation about possibilities, we settled upon a book about Till's murder. Initially, my basic goal for writing the book was to provide an updated narrative of the case in light of new documentary narratives of the murder as well as new information culled from the Federal Bureau of Investigation's report that was published in 2008. With the sixtieth anniversary of the murder fast approaching in August 2015, we believed an updated narrative of the case would be a timely contribution.

However, with the publication and commercial success of Trevor Getz's *Abina and The Important Men: A Graphic History* (Oxford University Press, 2012), Wheel suggested that perhaps an updated narrative of the murder could be compellingly presented in a graphic history format. As someone who was an avid comic book collector in my childhood, I was immediately intrigued by the idea, and after a month of deliberating on the pros and cons of writing a graphic history, I decided to take the plunge.

Opting to write a graphic history instead of a standard text-based narrative of Till's murder forced me to have a deeper engagement with Till and the circumstances surrounding his murder. For instance, as I began to imagine story plot and dialogue, I was immediately confronted with a painful reality—Emmett Till did not leave behind, or better yet was not allowed to leave behind, a documentary record of his life. Because he was never able to sit for an interview or write a reflection on his life, everything we know about him is from the perspective of people who knew him. Therefore, my challenge became sifting through the myriad reflections and reminiscences about him in order to imagine what his authentic voice would have sounded like as well as the words he would have used to communicate his thoughts, feelings, and desires. To be sure, figuring out how he spoke or more broadly used language is not something that I would have necessarily pondered had I written a standard historical treatment of the murder, but nonetheless it became vitally important for me in crafting realistic scenes and dialogue that were representative of Till's personality and character.

The process of researching and imagining Till's personality helped me to realize that a deeper aim of the book had to be about emphasizing who he was in life and not simply the tragic set of circumstances that robbed him of life. With this context in mind, in the pages of the graphic history, I have aimed to bring to life the richness of his humanity. Through well-known and not-so-well-known stories told about him by his friends and family, I have aimed to reveal Till as a jovial, confident, compassionate, and even courageous young man. He had a zest for life and was beloved by all those who came to know him.

As such, my primary goal in writing the book shifted from simply telling the story of what happened to him to emphasizing who he was in life. In other words, my desire is for the book's readers to connect with Till as a three-dimensional human being rather than as a historical symbol or as the civil rights martyr that he became. For all these reasons, *The Murder of Emmett Till: A Graphic History* strives to be a tribute to an extraordinary young man who was taken from us too soon but continues to live on in our hearts and memories.

A NOTE ON RACIAL EPITHETS

In this graphic history, I have not shied away from employing racial epithets to depict anti-black hostility and the culture of white supremacy in
the American South. While I believe the use of racial epithets in everyday
discourse is offensive, they are nonetheless necessary for presenting a realistic historical portrayal. It should be noted that every use of a racial epithet
in the graphic history was carefully considered and judiciously deployed.
For audiences for whom the use of racial epithets is not age-appropriate or
is simply too disturbing, please allow this brief note to serve as a trigger
warning.

ACKNOWLEDGMENTS

Books are collaborative enterprises, and the creation of *The Murder of Emmett Till: A Graphic History* was certainly a case in point. There are always more people to thank than memory can serve; however, certain individuals' contributions to a book's creation leave an imprint on the book as well as the author. For this book, those individuals include Saad Abi-Hamad, Paul Bjerk, Manu Vimalassery, Sean Cunningham, Jacob Baum, Emily Skidmore, Aliza Wong, Stefano D'amico, Zach Brittsan, Chris Whitmore, John Stewart, Greg Graham, Jeanette Davidson, David Wrobel, Maurice Hobson, Sundiata Cha-Jua, David Roediger, Clarence Lang, James Stewart, and Peter Rachleff. In small and large ways, these individuals encouraged me to pursue the book when I was uncertain of whether I had the talent or temperament. They are great colleagues and even better people.

My academic coach and friend, Joy Howard, deserves special mention. In the three years that I've worked with her, she's helped me to transform my scholarly identity in ways that have allowed me to be more impactful and productive. Without her guidance this project may have never blossomed.

My graphic history would certainly not have been possible without Brian Wheel's vision. Although Brian was not able to see the project through as editor, he nonetheless made lasting contributions to the book's rationale and overall structure. My editor, Charles Cavaliere, came on board with the project several years after it began. Although there were many delays and missed deadlines along the way, he remained committed to me and the project. All authors should have an editor as patient and gracious as Charles.

The peer reviewers who read early drafts of the book provided invaluable feedback on many interpretative points and suggested pertinent historical documents to use. For their careful sleuthing, the book has greater clarity and focus. In addition to several anonymous reviewers, I'd like to thank the following instructors who reviewed this graphic history, either as an early proposal or a manuscript:

Susan Autry, Central Piedmont Community College
Michael Benjamin, Georgia Southern University
W. Marvin Dulaney, University of Texas, Arlington
Ashley Farmer, University of Texas at Austin
Angela Flounory, University of Michigan-Dearborn
Jeffrey D. Gonda, Syracuse University
Mark D. Higbee, Eastern Michigan University
Eric R. Jackson, Northern Kentucky University
Karen K. Miller, Boston College
Timothy B. Smith, University of Tennessee at Martin
John Howard Smith, Texas A&M University-Commerce
Jacobi Williams, Indiana University

In the final stages of revision, Dave Tell provided critical feedback that put my mind and spirit at ease. I hope one day I'm able to return the favor. Also, the University of Mississippi's *Graphic Novels and Comics Across the Humanities* conference in September 2019 inspired me to connect my work with scholars in other disciplines. Mary Thurlkill, organizer of the conference, is to be commended for her unique talents in building a community of scholars devoted to graphic storytelling. I'm appreciative she welcomed me into that community.

I want to thank my trusted research assistant, Kyla Lewis, for her talents at primary source transcription. In so many ways, Kyla is the book's guardian angel who stood ready to do whatever was necessary to assist its fledgling author. I'm indebted to her always.

Last but not least, I want to thank my artist, Dave Dodson, for the graphic history's beautiful artwork. The extent to which the story of Emmett Till comes alive on the pages of the graphic history is due to Dave's skill as an artist. I hope he's willing to work together again.

For my wife, Jennie Hill, and my twins, Nia and Nye Hill, thank you for providing the love and support that all writers need to start and finish a project that unfolds over many years.

To all those whose contributions I have inadvertently omitted, thanks for your support as well.

GRAPHIC HISTORY SERIES

Widely acclaimed by educators, the award-winning Graphic History Series introduces students to the ways that historians construct the past. Going beyond simply depicting events in the past, each title in the Graphic History series combines the power of imagery with primary sources, historical essays, and cutting-edge historiography to offer a powerful tool for teaching history and teaching *about* history.

PUBLISHED

Trevor R. Getz and Liz Clarke, *Abina and the Important Men*

Ronald Schechter and Liz Clark, *Mendoza the Jew: Boxing, Manliness, and Nationalism*

Rafe Blaufarb and Liz Clarke, *Inhuman Traffick: The International Struggle Against the Atlantic Slave Trade*

Nina Caputo and Liz Clarke, *Debating Truth: The Barcelona Disputation of 1263*

Andrew Kirk and Kristian Purcell, *Doom Towns: The People and Landscapes of Atomic Testing*

Michael G. Vann and Liz Clarke, *The Great Hanoi Rate Hunt: Empire, Race, and Modernity in French Colonial Vietnam*

Charles F. Walker and Liz Clarke, *Witness to the Age of Revolution: The Odyssey of Juan Bautista Tupac Amaru*

FORTHCOMING

Bryan McCann and Gilmar Fraga, *The Black Lancers and the Ragamuffin Revolt*

Maura Elizabeth Cunningham and Liz Clarke, *Wandering Lives: Art and Politics in Twentieth-Century China*

THE MURDER OF EMMETT TILL

PART I
THE GRAPHIC HISTORY

CHAPTER 1
THE WHISTLING INCIDENT

In 1924, when Mamie Carthan was two years old, her family left Mississippi for Argo, Illinois, a town 12 miles from Chicago. Like so many other black people leaving the South during the 1920's, the Carthan family hoped for a better life in the North.

In 1940, Mamie Carthan married Louis Till and a year later the couple gave birth to Emmett, who they nicknamed Bobo.

Chicago, Illinois, home of Mamie and Emmett Till. August 1955.

Mama, Wheeler is going to Mississippi with Papa Mose. Can I go, please, please?

By 1955, fourteen-year-old Emmett was an adventurous and fun-loving youth. Young Emmett loved to be the center of attention and he usually was.

Papa Mose or Moses Wright was Mamie's uncle. Papa Mose lived in Mississippi but was briefly visiting Chicago to attend a funeral. While in Chicago, Papa Mose lodged with his relative, Willie Mae.

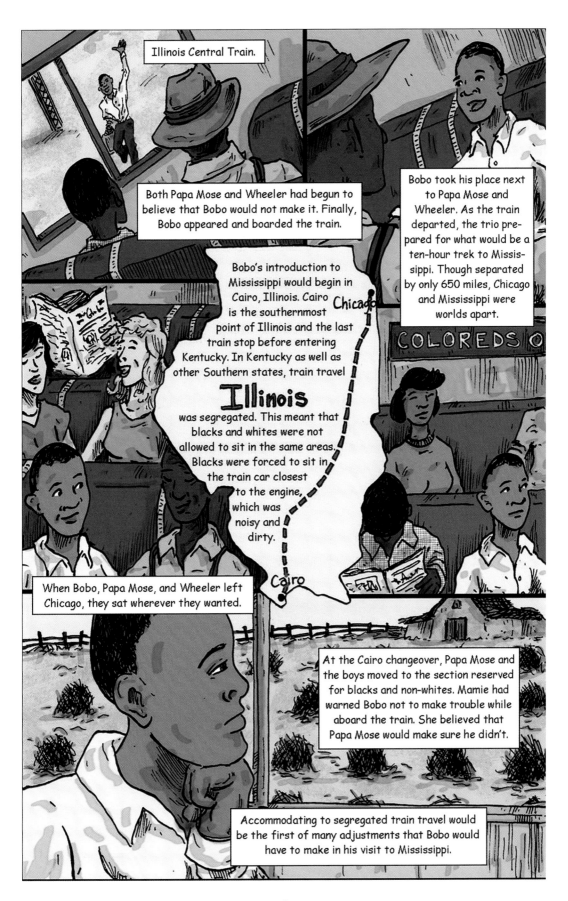

Illinois Central Train.

Both Papa Mose and Wheeler had begun to believe that Bobo would not make it. Finally, Bobo appeared and boarded the train.

Bobo took his place next to Papa Mose and Wheeler. As the train departed, the trio prepared for what would be a ten-hour trek to Mississippi. Though separated by only 650 miles, Chicago and Mississippi were worlds apart.

Bobo's introduction to Mississippi would begin in Cairo, Illinois. Cairo is the southernmost point of Illinois and the last train stop before entering Kentucky. In Kentucky as well as other Southern states, train travel

Illinois

was segregated. This meant that blacks and whites were not allowed to sit in the same areas. Blacks were forced to sit in the train car closest to the engine, which was noisy and dirty.

Chicago

Cairo

COLOREDS O

When Bobo, Papa Mose, and Wheeler left Chicago, they sat wherever they wanted.

At the Cairo changeover, Papa Mose and the boys moved to the section reserved for blacks and non-whites. Mamie had warned Bobo not to make trouble while aboard the train. She believed that Papa Mose would make sure he didn't.

Accommodating to segregated train travel would be the first of many adjustments that Bobo would have to make in his visit to Mississippi.

The Mississippi that Bobo arrived to was in turmoil. In May 1954, the U.S. Supreme Court had ruled that school desegregation was unconstitutional. Three months before Emmett arrived in Mississippi, the high court ruled that segregated school districts must desegregate "with all deliberate speed."

Many white Southerners and especially white Mississippians interpreted the Supreme Court ruling as an attack on their way of life. Across Mississippi, White Citizens' Councils and Klu Klux Klan chapters mobilized to prevent desegregation.

A few months before Emmett arrived in Mississippi, black civil rights activists Lamar Smith and Reverend George Washington Lee were brutally murdered for helping black Mississippians register to vote.

Indeed, black life was cheap in Mississippi and even cheaper when blacks directly or indirectly challenged the status quo. In Mississippi between 1877 and 1950, white mobs lynched 654 black people and 18 of those individuals had been lynched in Leflore County, Mississippi.

Leflore County was situated in the northwestern section of Mississippi, or the Mississippi Delta region. Historians have referred to the Mississippi Delta as "the most Southern place on earth" owing to its reputation of having the most rigid segregation and hostile black-white relations in the South.

MISSISSIPPI RIVER

MISSISSIPPI Delta

It was in Leflore County, Mississippi, that Bobo would spend his two-week summer vacation.

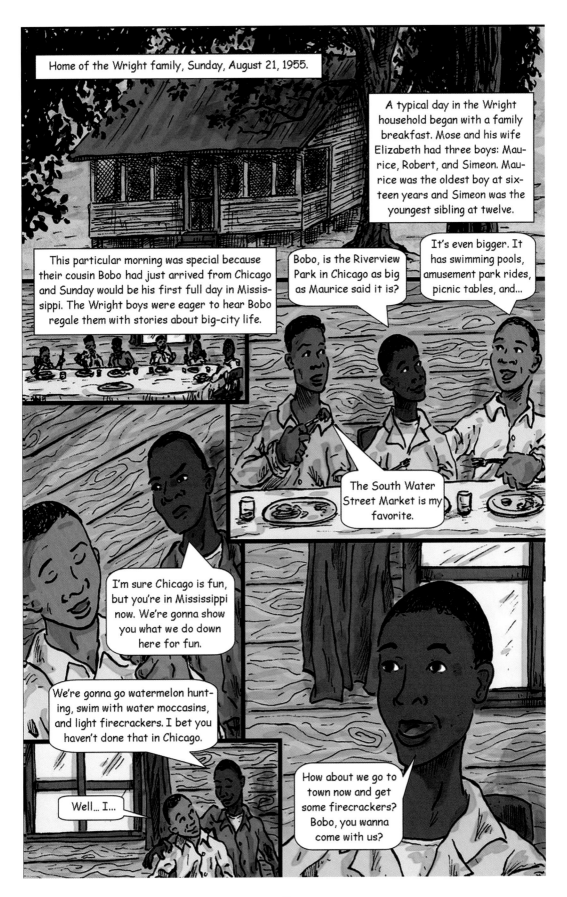

Grover Frederick Plantation, Monday, August 22, 1955.

Papa Mose and his family were share-croppers on the Grover Frederick Plantation. Typically, sharecroppers resided on a plantation and farmed the plantation owner's land in exchange for a portion of cotton sales.

In the Mississippi Delta, cotton was king and Bobo's arrival coincided with the beginning of cotton picking season.

Cotton picking was arduous work and not for the faint of heart. In late August in the Delta, temperatures soared to the mid-90's. On the Grover Frederick Plantation as well as many other plantations throughout the South, cotton was still picked by hand.

Bobo had received a nine-foot sack from Papa Mose and was told to fill it with cotton. Most boys Bobo's age could fill three nine-foot sacks in a day. Since this represented Bobo's first attempt at picking cotton, Maurice and Simeon took it upon themselves to teach Bobo a thing or two.

Bobo was completely unprepared for what awaited him in the cotton fields. He stood out like a sore thumb. Instead of overalls or blue jeans like the other boys, Bobo wore khaki slacks and penny loafers. Bobo was fond of wearing hats, so he wore one of his favorites to protect himself from the sun's glare.

Bobo made a good start of it but after about a half hour, sweat poured down his brow and his cotton picking slowed to a snail-like pace. At weighing-up time, Bobo had maybe a quarter of his cotton sack filled.

Now Bobo, the key to picking cotton is pulling out the cotton boll without any of the debris.

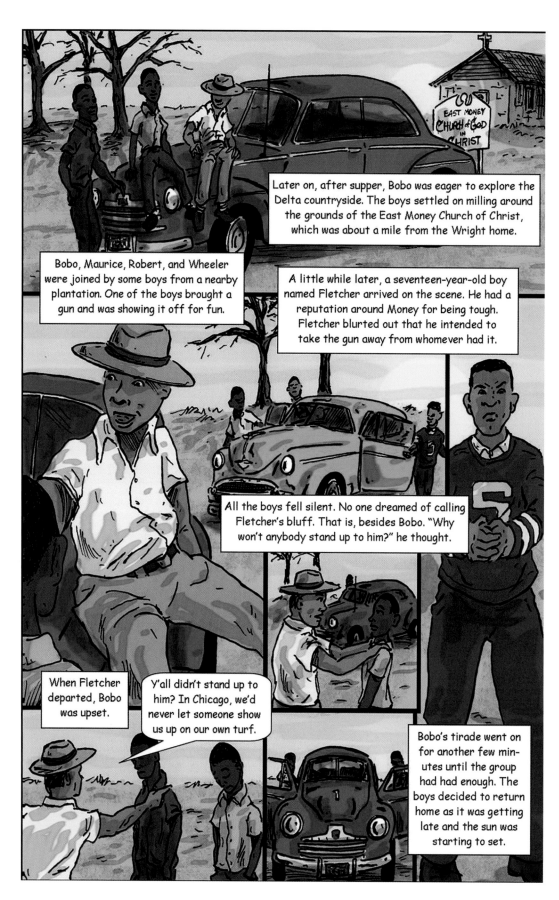

Later on, after supper, Bobo was eager to explore the Delta countryside. The boys settled on milling around the grounds of the East Money Church of Christ, which was about a mile from the Wright home.

Bobo, Maurice, Robert, and Wheeler were joined by some boys from a nearby plantation. One of the boys brought a gun and was showing it off for fun.

A little while later, a seventeen-year-old boy named Fletcher arrived on the scene. He had a reputation around Money for being tough. Fletcher blurted out that he intended to take the gun away from whomever had it.

All the boys fell silent. No one dreamed of calling Fletcher's bluff. That is, besides Bobo. "Why won't anybody stand up to him?" he thought.

When Fletcher departed, Bobo was upset.

Y'all didn't stand up to him? In Chicago, we'd never let someone show us up on our own turf.

Bobo's tirade went on for another few minutes until the group had had enough. The boys decided to return home as it was getting late and the sun was starting to set.

Home of the Wright family, Tuesday, August 23, 1955.

The cotton fields were a baptism by fire for Bobo. It was an experience that he was not in a hurry to repeat.

Bobo had convinced Aunt Lizzy to allow him to stay home rather than go into the cotton fields on Tuesday.

One of the biggest jobs was washing clothes. The Wright's had a Maytag wringer washing machine. Bobo had a similar washing machine at his home in Chicago, so he knew how to operate it.

Aunt Lizzy conferred with Papa Mose. Since this was Bobo's vacation, Papa Mose agreed to let him stay home and help Aunt Lizzy around the house.

When the washing had been completed, Bobo helped Aunt Lizzy pick vegetables from the family garden.

Aunt Lizzy tried to keep Bobo busy with chores but he quickly became bored. He daydreamed about going swimming with his cousins after they returned home from picking cotton.

15

When Maurice, Robert, Simeon, and Wheeler returned from the cotton fields on Wednesday afternoon, they were spent. But after spending yet another day inside doing house chores, Bobo was brimming with energy. He wanted to get out of the house. So in order to appease Bobo, the boys decided to venture into Money. They decided they would pick up some candy and soda at the Bryant's Grocery and Meat Market.

Wednesday, August 24, 1955.

When the boys arrived, they noticed that there were two older black men playing checkers outside.

Simeon was the first to go into the grocery to get some candy.

After Simeon returned, Bobo went inside.

Maurice remembered Bobo's firecracker incident and wanted to make sure nothing like that happened this time. "Simeon, go check on Bobo."

Being a dutiful younger brother, Simeon went inside the grocery to check on Bobo.

Carolyn Bryant and her husband, Roy Bryant, were the owners of the grocery. The store catered to black sharecroppers in the area. When the boys visited the grocery, Carolyn Bryant was alone in the store as Roy Bryant was away on a trip.

After a few minutes of wandering through the store, Bobo purchased two cents' worth of candy from Carolyn Bryant.

CHAPTER 2
THE KIDNAPPING

However, Roosevelt Crawford had not been so discreet. He relayed to his family Bobo's indiscretion and they became alarmed.

Simmy, I heard what happened at the Bryants' store yesterday. Did Bobo really whistle at that white woman?

We didn't know he would do that.

Y'all gonna hear about this again. I know them white folks—they some mean peckerwoods.

Papa Mose know about all this?

You best tell your daddy to get Bobo outta Money on the first train.

Even after Ruth Crawford's plea to get Emmett out of town, neither Simeon, Maurice, Robert, nor Wheeler confessed to Papa Mose what had happened and what was brewing. The boys stayed silent because they didn't want to get Emmett in trouble and more importantly they didn't want to see him sent home.

Worried that Bobo might be in some danger, Ruth Crawford's mother paid a visit to Elizabeth Wright.

Lizzy, I hear your boy Bobo got into some trouble in Money … you know about that?

23

Bryant's Grocery and Meat Market, Saturday, August 27, 1955.

It had been several days since Emmett whistled at Carolyn Bryant. In the meantime, Roy Bryant, her husband, had returned home.

Upon his return, Carolyn didn't divulge the incident between her and Emmett. Rather, he learned of it secondhand. Having to find out in this way that his wife had been accosted angered him.

Why didn't you tell me what happened? Everybody in this town knows what happened except me!

I'm sorry, Roy. I knew if I told you, you would go and make trouble.

All you've done is made me mad. The damn ni**er is gonna pay!

With rumors of the incident circulating, Roy Bryant felt he had to act. In fact, white supremacy demanded it. Any white man worth his salt could not let a black male threaten his family and get away with it. A white man who failed to defend white womanhood and particularly his wife's honor would be treated by other whites as a race traitor and coward.

With all these thoughts swirling in Roy Bryant's head, he became filled with paranoia, rage, and a desire for revenge.

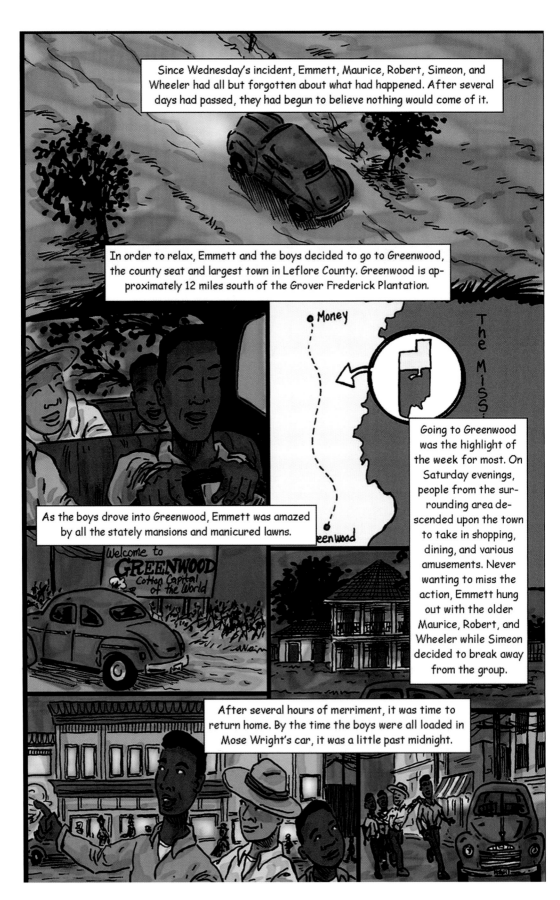

Since Wednesday's incident, Emmett, Maurice, Robert, Simeon, and Wheeler had all but forgotten about what had happened. After several days had passed, they had begun to believe nothing would come of it.

In order to relax, Emmett and the boys decided to go to Greenwood, the county seat and largest town in Leflore County. Greenwood is approximately 12 miles south of the Grover Frederick Plantation.

Money

The Miss.

Going to Greenwood was the highlight of the week for most. On Saturday evenings, people from the surrounding area descended upon the town to take in shopping, dining, and various amusements. Never wanting to miss the action, Emmett hung out with the older Maurice, Robert, and Wheeler while Simeon decided to break away from the group.

As the boys drove into Greenwood, Emmett was amazed by all the stately mansions and manicured lawns.

Welcome to GREENWOOD Cotton Capital of the World

eenwood

After several hours of merriment, it was time to return home. By the time the boys were all loaded in Mose Wright's car, it was a little past midnight.

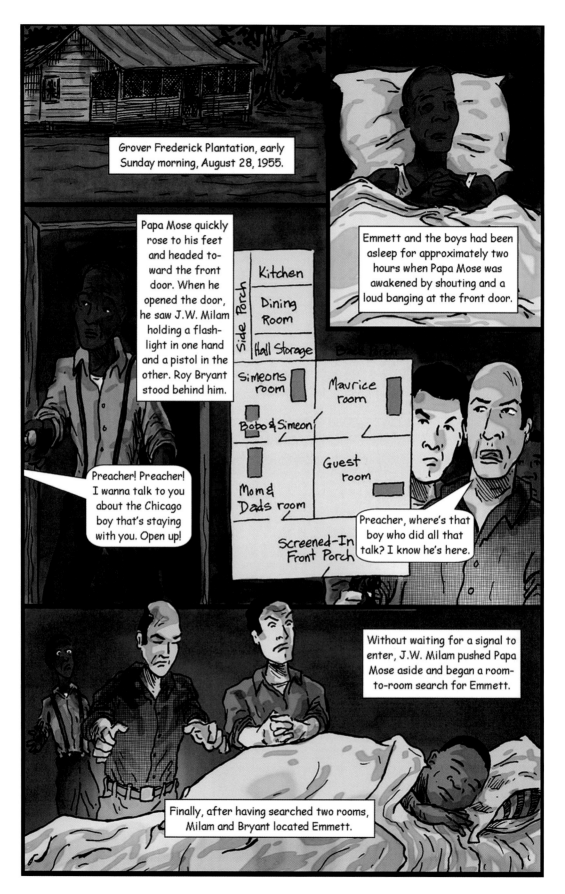

Grover Frederick Plantation, early Sunday morning, August 28, 1955.

Emmett and the boys had been asleep for approximately two hours when Papa Mose was awakened by shouting and a loud banging at the front door.

Papa Mose quickly rose to his feet and headed toward the front door. When he opened the door, he saw J.W. Milam holding a flashlight in one hand and a pistol in the other. Roy Bryant stood behind him.

Preacher! Preacher! I wanna talk to you about the Chicago boy that's staying with you. Open up!

Preacher, where's that boy who did all that talk? I know he's here.

Side Porch

Kitchen

Dining Room

Hall Storage

Bedroom

Simeons room

Maurice room

Bobo & Simeon

Guest room

Mom & Dads room

Screened-In Front Porch

Without waiting for a signal to enter, J.W. Milam pushed Papa Mose aside and began a room-to-room search for Emmett.

Finally, after having searched two rooms, Milam and Bryant located Emmett.

29

CHAPTER 3
THE MURDER

41

46

Several hours later. cemetery in Money, Mississippi.

Mose Wright and family had gathered at the funeral home. Emmett's body had been placed in a simple pine coffin. It lied on the ground near the hole that had been dug for the coffin. A minister read Emmett Till's eulogy.

Stop the burial. The boy's mama wants the body shipped back to Chicago on the next train outta here.

In the interim, Mamie Till had contacted various Chicago authorities and convinced them to intervene on her behalf to stop Emmett's burial.

Chicago, Illinois. Friday, September 2nd.

Emmett Till's body was recovered from the train station and brought to the Rayner Funeral Home.

Mamie Till came to the funeral home to see her Bobo and make funeral preparations.

Well hold on, Mamie. I got a letter here that says this box cannot be opened under any circumstances.

Mr. Rayner, I need you to open that box so I can see my boy.

Okay. Okay. Slow down. I'll open the box but I need you to wait outside. When I pry it open, I'll fetch you.

If I have to pry this box open myself, I'm gonna see my son.

A.A. Rayner summons some workers to help him open the coffin.

Roberts Temple, Chicago, Illinois. Sunday, September 4th.

Masses of people and media were in attendance at the funeral.

True to her word, Mamie Till did not allow the funeral director to fix Bobo's face. Courageously, she decided to have an open-casket funeral and allowed the media to take pictures of Bobo's disfigured face.

CHAPTER 4
THE TRIAL AND AFTERMATH

OWN THE CURTA

RACIST TERROR IN MISSISSIPPI

EMMETT TILL WAS MURDERED

AMERICA DEMANDS EQUAL RIGHTS for NEGROES

Protests erupted nationwide.

1955

WA021 PD

the White House
Washington
1955 SEP 2 PM 7 17

M
WA020 PD
FC CHICAGO ILL SEP 2 307PMC
THE PRESIDENT
THE WHITE HOUSE
I THE MOTHER OF EMMETT TILL AM PLEADING THAT
PERSONALLY SEE THAT JUSTICE IS METED OUT TO ALL
INVOLVED IN THE BEASTLY LYNCHING OF MY SON IN MON
MISS. AWAITING A DIRECT REPLY FROM YOU
MAMIE TILL 1626 WEST 14TH PLCH

8-0654

Mamie Till appeals to President Eisenhower to open a federal investigation into Emmett Till's murder. President Eisenhower refuses to read the telegram.

Two months after the Emmett Till murder trial, a Mississippi grand jury chose not to indict J.W. Milam and Roy Bryant on kidnapping charges connected with the Emmett Till murder case.

Four months after the end of the Emmett Till murder trial, J.W. Milam and Roy Bryant went on record to a reporter that the two men had in fact killed Emmett Till. Milam and Bryant's lawyers provided the reporter with a story that portrayed Emmett Till as defiant and boastful about his exploits with white women. In exchange for the fabricated story, both Milam and Bryant received a cash payment.

Mister, mister ... read all about it. New details on the Emmett Till murder case.

Look magazine cover, January 1956: "The Shocking Story of An Approved Killing in Mississippi"

In 2008, Carolyn Bryant revealed that Emmett Till had not accosted her during their encounter in the store or made lewd comments to her.

Nothing that boy did could ever justify what happened to him.

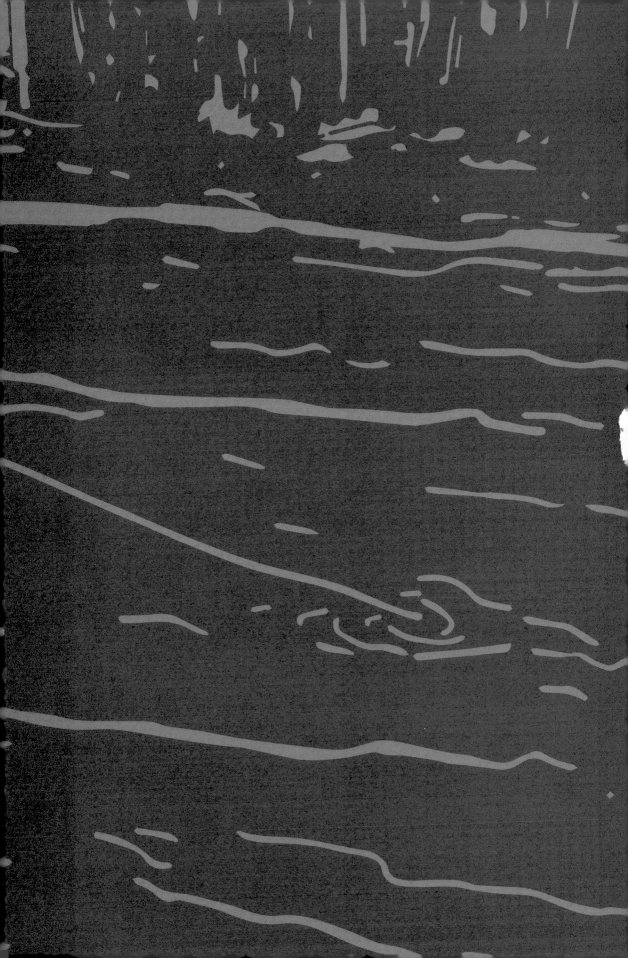

PART II
THE HISTORICAL CONTEXT

THE MISSISSIPPI DELTA AND THE CULTURE OF SOUTHERN SEGREGATION

In the 1896 *Plessy v. Ferguson* decision, the U.S. Supreme Court ruled that it was lawful to separate black and white public accommodations as long as they were equal. The *Plessy* decision set in motion *de jure* segregation—a wave of exclusionary policies in which Southern state and local governments passed hundreds of legal statutes that excluded or separated blacks and whites in public and private life. For example, segregation laws prohibited blacks and whites from attending the same schools, eating at the same restaurants, drinking from the same water fountains, or receiving care at the same hospitals. In facilities in which blacks were not expressly prohibited, they were forced to enter through the back door or sit in separate areas designated for their race. Although the *Plessy* ruling specified that black and white accommodations had to be equal in order to be constitutional, in practice black accommodations were patently inferior or nonexistent. By the 1920s, every Southern state government had passed laws segregating blacks and whites.[1]

While there were numerous segregation laws that regulated the interaction of blacks and whites in public space, segregation extended far beyond formal law. *De jure* segregation was undergirded by racial etiquette, which refers to a myriad of informal and unspoken rules that governed the interpersonal interactions between blacks and whites. White Southerners required blacks to refer to them at all times as "sir" or "miss," even if the person being addressed was a child. Alternatively, regardless of the age or stature of a black man or woman, white Southerners referred to black men as "boy" and black women as "auntie." When a black person encountered a white Southerner on a sidewalk, the black person was required to step off the sidewalk until the white person had passed. Only then could the black person get back on the sidewalk and resume their

---

1   For an in-depth treatment of segregation practices in the South, see Leon Litwack, *Trouble in Mind: Black Southerners in the Age of Jim Crow* (New York: Random House, 1999), especially 229–246.

journey. When purchasing an item from a white-owned store, blacks had to be careful not to touch the hand of the white clerk when exchanging money. Doing so was a sign of black insolence. White Southerners judged black people as uppity or not knowing their place if they looked directly into the eyes of a white person. For black men, even looking in the direction of a white woman was as a lynchable offense.[2]

In 1955, Emmett Till was not simply traveling to the segregated South; he was traveling to Money, Mississippi. Money, which lies in the heart of the Mississippi Delta, was perhaps the worst place for the young, capricious, and confident Till to visit during the summer of 1955. The Delta, as it is commonly referred to, is located in the northwest section of Mississippi, or the state's historic plantation district. In the 1950s, blacks represented more than half of the Delta's population, yet whites controlled all aspects of life and especially economic life.[3] For Delta whites, Jim Crow segregation was not simply a way of life—it *was* life. The passion with which Delta whites adhered to white supremacy earned it the reputation as the "most Southern place on Earth."[4] This moniker spoke to the extent to which Delta whites ruthlessly pursued the suppression of black economic independence as well as black political participation. Segregationists believed that any amount of black economic and political self-determination would inevitably lead to social equality and, worst of all, intermarriage between the races. If social equality was tolerated, the white race would disappear due to "mongrelization," or the intermixing of white and non-white bloodlines. In a subculture devoted to maintaining white supremacy and white blood purity, even a black child's whistle at a white woman was enough to incite white fears of racial dissolution.

LYNCHING AND RACIAL VIOLENCE IN THE SOUTH

White Southerners violently enforced both the formal and unspoken rules of Jim Crow segregation. Any black person refusing to comply with segregation ordinances or racial etiquette could anticipate verbal threats, acts of intimidation, economic reprisals, beatings, or lynching. Additionally, black women were raped by white men frequently during the Jim Crow era. White-on-black rape powerfully demonstrated white men's unfettered

---

2   Ibid., 34–47.

3   Ibid., 122.

4   For a rich interpretation of the culture of segregation in the Mississippi Delta, see James E. Cobb, *The Most Southern Place on Earth: The Mississippi Delta and the Roots of Regional Identity* (New York: Oxford University Press, 1994), in particular 147–177.

access to black female bodies and their masculine and sexual dominance over black men.[5] Of the various forms of intimidation and coercion employed to terrorize black Americans, lynching was perhaps the most spectacular and brutal. While definitions of lynching vary, at the core lynchings were public murders carried out by a group of vigilantes for the purpose of summarily punishing an alleged criminal or perceived social deviant. Lynch mobs mutilated, burned alive, dragged to death, shot to death, and hung lynch victims from trees. Lynchings took place in rural areas and in crowded downtowns. Hundreds and sometimes thousands of spectators gathered to witness the lynching of a black person. Afterwards, white spectators might purchase a photograph of the lynching as a keepsake.[6] Although lynchings were meant to terrorize black Americans into accepting segregation, black Americans protested lynchings and organized a four-decades-long movement to secure federal antilynching legislation.[7]

White-on-black lynchings were most common during the years 1870 and 1950. During this period, approximately 5,000 documented lynchings occurred in the South, 654 in Mississippi alone.[8] While all black people (specifically women, children, and the elderly) were potential targets of white lynch mob violence, black men constituted nearly 90 percent of total lynchings.[9] White lynchers offered a litany of reasons for lynching a

5   For an overview of the long history of white male rape against black women in the twentieth century and the anti-rape campaigns to combat it, see Danielle L. McGuire, *At the Dark End of The Street: Black Women, Rape, and Resistance—A New History of the Civil Rights Movement from Rosa Parks to the Rise of Black Power* (New York: Knopf, 2010), especially 28–30. For a comprehensive analysis of post–Civil War sexual violence against black women, see Hannah Rosen, *Terror in the Heart of Freedom: Citizenship, Sexual Violence, and the Meaning of Race in the Post-Emancipation South* (Chapel Hill: University of North Carolina Press, 2009).

6   For an in-depth treatment of lynchings as modern spectacles, see Amy Louise Wood, *Lynching and Spectacle: Witnessing Racial Violence in America, 1890–1940* (Chapel Hill: University of North Carolina Press, 2009).

7   Scholarship on the quest for federal antilynching legislation includes Donald L. Grant, *The Anti-Lynching Movement, 1883–1932* (San Francisco: R and E Research Associates, 1975); Jacqueline Dowd Hall, *Revolt Against Chivalry: Jesse Daniel Ames and the Women's Campaign Against Lynching* (New York: Columbia University Press, 1979); Robert Zangrando, *The NAACP Crusade Against Lynching, 1909–1950* (Philadelphia: Temple University Press, 1980); Patricia Bernstein, *The First Waco Horror: The Lynching of Jesse Washington and the Rise of the NAACP* (College Station: Texas A&M Press, 2006); and Christopher Waldrep, *African Americans Confront Lynching: Strategies of Resistance from the Civil War to the Civil Rights Era* (New York: Rowman and Littlefield, 2009).

8   For the most up-to-date statistics on Southern lynching, see Equal Justice Initiative, "Lynching in America: Confronting the Legacy of Racial Terror," accessed December 30, 2017, https://lynchinginamerica.eji.org/report/#lynching-in-america.

9   Stewart E. Tolnay and Amy K. Bailey, *Lynched: The Victims of Southern Mob Violence* (Chapel Hill: University of North Carolina Press, 2015), 230.

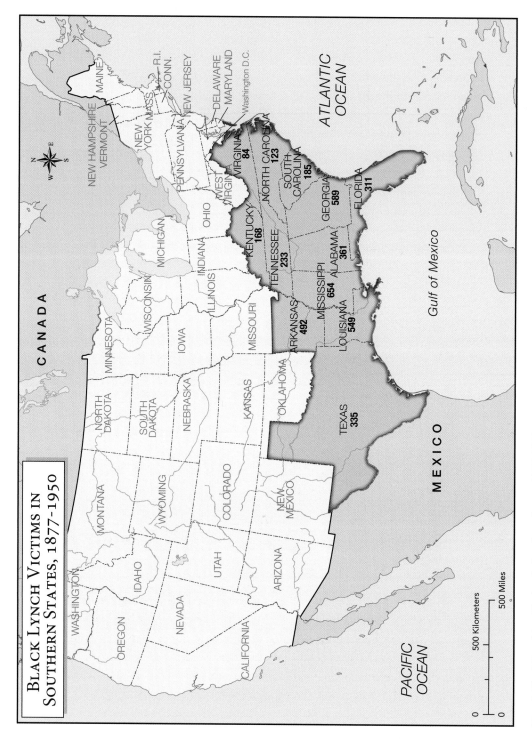

Map 1. Black Lynching Victims in Southern States, 1877–1950

TABLE 1. REASONS GIVEN FOR LYNCHING OF BLACKS, 1882–1930

Acting suspiciously	Grave robbing	Race hatred
Adultery	Improper with white woman	Race troubles
Aiding murderer	Incest	Rape
Arguing with white man	Inciting to riot	Rape-murders
Arson	Inciting trouble	Resisting mob
Assassination	Indolence	Revenge
Attempted murder	Inflammatory language	Robbery
Banditry	Informing	Running a bordello
Being disreputable	Injuring livestock	Sedition
Being obnoxious	Insulting white man	Slander
Boasting about riot	Insulting white woman	Spreading Disease
Burglary	Insurrection	Stealing
Child abuse	Kidnapping	Suing white man
Conjuring	Killing livestock	Swindling
Courting white woman	Living with white woman	Terrorism
Criminal assault	Looting	Testifying against white man
Cutting levee	Making threats	Throwing stones
Defending rapist	Miscegenation	Train wrecking
Demanding respect	Mistaken identity	Trying to colonize blacks
Disorderly conduct	Molestation	Trying to vote
Eloping with white woman	Murder	Unpopularity
Entered white woman's room	Nonsexual assault	Unruly remarks
Enticement	Peeping Tom	Using obscene language
Extortion	Pillage	Vagrancy
Fraud	Plotting to kill	Violated quarantine
Frightening white woman	Poisoning well	Voodooism
Gambling	Quarreling	Voting for wrong party

Source: Stewart Tolnay and E.M. Beck, *Festival of Violence: An Analysis of Southern Lynchings, 1882–1930,* (Urbana: University of Illinois Press, 1995), 47.

black person, such as talking back to a white person, demanding respect, and being obnoxious.[10] However, the alleged murder of a white person accounted for approximately 40 percent of allegations that precipitated white-on-black lynchings and the alleged rape of a white woman by a black man for approximately 20 percent.[11] In the white imagination, white-on-black lynchings was the only effective means of deterring black

---

10   Ibid., 231–233.

11   Equal Justice Initiative, "Lynching in America."

sexual predators or "black beast rapists" from sexual crimes against white woman. Proponents of lynching asserted that the formal criminal justice system was slow and unpredictable and furthermore could not be trusted to protect the community from black criminality. Only the white population and its best citizens could be trusted to do so, and only swift and brutal punishment could act as a deterrent to black criminality and especially sexual violence against white women.[12] Thus, when J. W. Milam and Roy Bryant decided to torture and murder Till for whistling at Carolyn Bryant, they believed they were acting in the interest of protecting white womanhood.

THE GREAT MIGRATION

Why was Emmett Till, a Chicago native, visiting Money, Mississippi, in the summer of 1955? Well before Till was born, his mother, Mamie, and her immediate family left Mississippi for Argo, Illinois (a suburb of Chicago), in 1921.[13] Black people affectionately referred to Argo as "Little Mississippi" because of the large number of black migrants from Mississippi who settled there.[14] The family's departure from Mississippi was a part of a much larger black exodus from the South that is commonly referred to as the Great Migration. In 1900, more than 90 percent of black Americans resided in the Southern United States. However, between 1910 and 1970, more than six million black people left the South for the West, Midwest, and Northeastern United States. By 1970, more than 50 percent of black Americans lived outside the South.[15]

The vast majority of black Southerners migrated from the rural South to urban-industrial centers such as Chicago, Detroit, Cleveland, Los Angeles, New York City, Philadelphia, and Boston. Northern cities attracted black Americans for a variety of reasons, not the least being the availability of

---

12   Jacqueline Dowd Hall, "The Mind That Burns in Each Body: Women, Rape, and Racial Violence," *Southern Exposure* 12 (1984): 61–71; Michael Pfeifer, *Rough Justice: Lynching and American Society, 1874–1947* (Urbana: University of Illinois Press, 2006), 3.

13   For the sake of consistency and clarity, I refer to Till's mother as Mamie Till (throughout the graphic history and historical context/documents sections) even though she was referred to as Mamie Bradley during the murder trial and in contemporaneous press accounts.

14   Christopher Benson, *The Death of Innocence: The Story of the Hate Crime That Changed America* (New York: Random House, 2004), 44. This is perhaps the best telling of the Till murder saga from the vantage point of Mamie Till.

15   One of the most comprehensive presentations of the history and significance of the Great Migration is Isabel Wilkerson, *The Warmth of Other Suns: The Epic Story of America's Great Migration* (New York: Vintage, 2010), specifically 21–25.

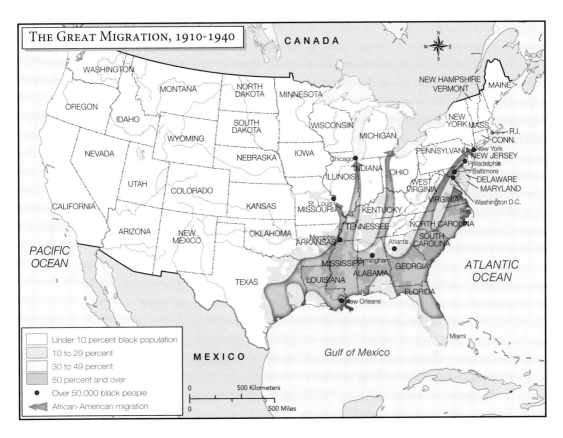

Map 2. The Great Migration, 1910–1940

higher-paying industrial wage work. Moreover, the Northern United States and especially urban-industrial centers offered black Americans a reprieve from the South's repressive racial caste system.[16] For these reasons, Mamie Till's family, like millions of black Southerners, migrated north.

While several members of Mamie Till's extended family eventually moved to Chicago, the bulk remained in Mississippi. During summers, and especially after Emmett was born in 1941, Mamie Till returned to Mississippi with her son to visit relatives. Before 1955, Emmett Till had visited Mississippi on four separate occasions. On previous occasions, his mother had accompanied him.[17] Mamie Till hoped that visiting relatives in Mississippi would allow her son to develop close bonds with extended family. In fact, traveling back to

16   Ibid.

17   Perhaps the most exhaustively researched and comprehensive analysis of the Till murder case is Devery Anderson, *Emmett Till: The Murder That Shocked the World and Sparked the Civil Rights Movement* (Jackson: University of Mississippi Press, 2015). For a discussion of Mamie and Emmett Till's previous trips to the Mississippi Delta, see Anderson, *Emmett Till*, 14.

the South in the summer was a normal, even expected, occurrence for black families who had migrated north. So when fourteen-year-old Emmett Till set off for Money, Mississippi, in the summer of 1955, his mother believed she was doing her best to expose her son to his ancestral roots.

CIVIL RIGHTS ACTIVISM IN MISSISSIPPI

Of the numerous forms of discrimination black Americans faced, perhaps the one hardest to stomach was disenfranchisement, which refers to denying black people the right to vote. Throughout the South and especially in Mississippi, blacks had not exercised the right to vote since the 1890s. Disenfranchisement was stark in the Mississippi Delta. Although blacks accounted for 70 percent of the Delta's population in 1940, they represented less than 1 percent of registered voters. In fact, some majority-black Delta counties did not have one registered black voter.[18] White politicians asserted that voter registration among blacks was low because black people simply did not want to vote. However, nothing could have been farther from the truth: black Southerners desired to vote, but a variety of barriers, such as understanding clauses, literacy tests, and poll taxes, as well as outright violence and intimidation, kept blacks from registering.

During the 1940s and early 1950s, a small but well-organized cadre of black Mississippians sought to challenge disenfranchisement. In order to undermine the idea that black people did not want to vote or understand the value of voting, black activists organized voter registration drives throughout the state. Registration drives were housed at churches and other community centers in the black community. From the outset, black activists attempting to register black voters were verbally and physically threatened. Nonetheless, they refused to be intimidated and persisted in mobilizing black voters.[19]

In 1954, the *Brown v. Board of Education* ruling by the U.S. Supreme Court made school segregation illegal. The *Brown* decision invalidated the 1896 *Plessy* decision by decreeing that "separate but equal" public accommodations were unconstitutional. The *Brown* decision, perhaps more than any other court decision in American history, buoyed black optimism that racial change could occur even in the "Solid South," which had long been viewed as a region impervious to progressive social change. Moreover, the *Brown* decision galvanized civil rights organizations and

---

18   For one of the best analyses of black civil rights activism in the Mississippi Delta, see David Beito and Linda Beito, *Black Maverick: T.R.M. Howard's Fight for Civil Rights and Economic Power* (Urbana: University of Illinois Press, 2009), 45.

19   Ibid., 69–89.

spurred fundraising campaigns to challenge segregation in all realms of Southern life. Till's summer visit to Mississippi coincided with a rising tide of black activism—and a mounting white backlash in opposition to it.

MASSIVE RESISTANCE

In the wake of the *Brown* decision, a white supremacist reawakening occurred throughout the South, especially in the Deep South. In Mississippi, pro-segregation organizations such as the Ku Klux Klan vowed to block desegregation and voter registration efforts tooth and nail. For instance, the Mississippi-based Klan orchestrated dozens of church bombings, beatings of black sharecroppers, and killings of black activists attempting to register black voters. Additionally, new white supremacist organizations like the White Citizens' Council of America were founded days after the *Brown* decision. Whereas the Klan employed violence and intimidation, Mississippi-based White Citizens' Councils, which were composed mostly of the Southern white elite, used their personal and professional networks to petition white businessmen and government officials to resist federal efforts to implement school desegregation. Together, the Klan and White Citizens' Councils acted as an effective one–two punch against efforts to dismantle segregation.[20] The clash between black activists demanding equality and white segregationists' desire to maintain the racial status quo created deep ruptures in Southern society. When Emmett Till arrived in Money in the summer of 1955, Mississippi and the South was at a breaking point. Little did Till know that his summer visit would exacerbate those tensions.

THE DECISION TO TRAVEL TO MISSISSIPPI

In August 1955, Moses ("Mose") Wright, Emmett Till's great-uncle, visited Chicago. At some point during Wright's visit, Till learned that his cousins, Wheeler Parker and Curtis Jones, were going to travel with "Uncle Mose" back to Money for a couple of weeks. Till decided that he ought to travel to

---

20   On the mobilization of white supremacist groups in the Delta and the South in response to the *Brown v. Board of Education* decision, see Cobb, *The Most Southern Place on Earth*, Chapter 9, and Timothy Tyson, *The Blood of Emmett Till* (New York: Simon & Schuster, 2017), especially Chapter 10. Among the many contributions Tyson makes in *Blood of Emmet Till* is how he infers Emmett Till's awareness of white racism by describing how Till would have had to negotiate Chicago's racially segregated neighborhoods as well as the white terrorist violence that maintained them. In doing so, Tyson dispels the myth of fourteen-year-old Till as someone who would have been oblivious to the kind of white racism he encountered in the Mississippi Delta. For Tyson's full explanation, see *Blood of Emmett Till*, 14–16.

Mississippi as well, but his mother had other ideas. She initially refused his request because she had always traveled with him to Mississippi and was afraid of what might happen to him in her absence. Before allowing her son to leave, Mamie Till explained to him how Mississippi was different from Chicago. She emphasized that in the Mississippi, black people, especially black men and boys, had to be careful not to offend white people. She counseled her son that black men and boys had lost their lives just for looking at white women or even accidentally bumping into a white woman. She stressed to him that if he drew the ire of a white person, he should quickly apologize and even get on his hands and knees, if necessary. After having multiple talks about navigating the treacherous world of Southern race relations, Mamie Till felt a bit more at ease in allowing her son to travel to Mississippi without her. In order to further reassure her, Mose Wright promised that he would keep him safe. On this condition, Mamie Till relented and allowed her son to travel to Money for a two-week vacation.[21]

THE WHISTLING INCIDENT

On the evening of Wednesday, August 28, 1955, Emmett Till, Simeon Wright, Maurice Wright, Robert Wright, Wheeler Parker, and at least one other person piled into Mose Wright's 1946 Chevrolet truck and headed for Money. After a long hot summer day, Till and his cousins wanted to buy some cold sodas and candy. On this evening, the only convenience store still open was Bryant's Grocery and Meat Market. Till was the first of the group to venture inside; the rest waited outside. After a few moments, someone in the group encouraged Simeon Wright to go in after Till to make sure he didn't get into any trouble. Simeon Wright obliged. According to Simeon Wright, he witnessed Till buy some candy from Carolyn Bryant without incident. After doing so, Till and Simeon Wright walked out of the store together. A few moments later, Carolyn Bryant exited the store and Till whistled.[22] Both Simeon Wright and Wheeler Parker have repeatedly confirmed that Till did in fact whistle at or in the direction of Carolyn Bryant as she exited the store.[23] What remains a mystery is why he did so. According to Parker and Wright, no one in their group put Till up to whistling. Moreover,

---

21   Benson, *Death of Innocence*, 163.

22   Simeon Wright, *Simeon's Story: An Eyewitness Account of the Kidnapping of Emmett Till* (Chicago: Chicago Review Press, 2011), 33–35.

23   Simeon Wright interview, interviewed by Joseph Mosnier, Chicago, Illinois, May 23, 2011, transcript, Civil Rights History Project Collection, American Folklife Center, Library of Congress, Washington, DC; Wheeler Parker interview, interviewed by Joseph Mosnier, Chicago, Illinois, May 23, 2011, transcript, Civil Rights History Project Collection, American Folklife Center, Library of Congress, Washington, DC.

not only did he seemingly act without prodding, Parker and Wright assert that he whistled without the slightest indication or warning that he was going to do so. For all these reasons, when Till whistled at Carolyn Bryant, the group panicked and fled before the situation could escalate.[24]

The whistling incident was not the first time that Till had made an outburst or did something that his cousins did not anticipate. Parker recalled one such incident when he visited Till in Chicago. Parker recalled that he and Till were casually walking through a neighborhood when Till unexpectedly yelled to onlookers, "I've got my two big cousins here from Argo, Illinois, and can't nobody beat them up."[25] Frightened by the assertion and knowing that tough talk could get you beat up or worse in Chicago, Parker recalled having to "grab him real quick" before Till got them killed. Parker explained the outburst as part of Till's prankster nature. Additionally, Simeon Wright recalled that a few days before Till's infamous whistle, he had drawn the ire of his cousins by lighting a firecracker in Money. Simeon Wright remembered that, out of the blue, Till had lit the firecracker and reveled at the bang that it made. His cousins scolded him for the behavior and reminded him that lighting firecrackers in Money was frowned upon.[26]

Given Till's penchant for pranks, he likely understood that whistling at a woman, especially a white woman, would get the attention of his peers. Like other pranks he had engaged in, gaining the attention of his friends or family was seemingly paramount and perhaps superseded the danger that might ensue. Several days after the whistling incident, Carolyn Bryant's husband, Roy Bryant, and his half-brother, J. W. Milam, would come to Mose Wright's home to exact revenge for the innocent but undue attention Till had paid to Carolyn Bryant.

THE KIDNAPPING AND MURDER

In the early twentieth century, a black boy in Mississippi would have been lynched in front of dozens and perhaps hundreds of white spectators for allegedly assaulting a white woman. Yet this did not happen in the case of Till. Instead, Roy Bryant, J. W. Milam, and as many as fourteen accomplices waited until the dead of night to kidnap and murder Till.[27] While it

---

24   Wright, *Simeon's Story*, 33–35.

25   Wheeler Parker interview, Civil Rights History Project Collection.

26   Simeon Wright interview, Civil Rights History Project Collection.

27   According to filmmaker Keith Beauchamp, there is evidence to connect fourteen people with Till's kidnapping and murder. In 2005, Beauchamp claimed that as many of five of the fourteen were still alive. For a more detailed discussion of Beauchamp's claims, see Anderson, *Emmett Till*, 318.

is impossible to say for sure how many people participated in the kidnapping and murder conspiracy, Bryant and Milam's accomplices most likely included relatives (Carolyn Bryant, Leslie Milam, and Edward Milam), friends (Melvin Campbell, Hubert Clark, and Elmer Kimbell), and black laborers who worked for J. W. Milam (Henry Lee Loggins, Leroy "Too Tight" Collins, Otha "Oso" Johnson, and Joe Wille Hubbard).[28] Because it is impossible to establish with certainty the identities of the accomplices (with the exception of Leslie Milam, who admitted his complicity years later), the likely accomplices are unnamed and are represented as silhouettes in the graphic history.[29]

J. W. Milam, Roy Bryant, and their accomplices clandestinely kidnapped and murdered Till rather than orchestrating a lynching because lynchings were no longer publicly defensible. Since the 1930s, when the number of lynchings had declined to less than ten a year (down from a peak of more than one hundred per year in the 1890s), a lynching became a national news story as well as a Southern embarrassment.[30] Additionally, with nascent civil rights activists and organizations such as the National Association for the Advancement of Colored People (NAACP) skillfully drawing greater national and international attention to white abuses of black civil rights, white Southerners bent on preserving *de jure* segregation understood that wanton acts of violence that received coverage in the national media only brought undue attention to the region and could possibly make segregation more vulnerable to attack.[31] Therefore, rather than engage in highly visible acts like lynching, white Southerners such as J. W. Milam and Roy Bryant eschewed them in favor of verbal intimidation, beatings, and assassinations. Fearing that Mose Wright would divulge the kidnapping, J. W. Milam and Roy Bryant warned him that if he revealed what happened, they would kill him. After Milam, Bryant, and their accomplices killed Till, they hastily destroyed any physical evidence

---

28   For a detailed analysis of likely accomplices to the Till murder, see Anderson, *Emmett Till*, 368–377.

29   Prior to Leslie Milam's death in 1974, he confessed to his minister that he had been involved in the Till murder. See Anderson, *Emmett Till*, 334.

30   For an explanation of how and why Southern leaders and the Southern press increasingly condemned lynching in the post–World War I period, see Stewart E. Tolnay and E. M. Beck, *A Festival of Violence: An Analysis of Southern Lynchings, 1882–1930* (Urbana: University of Illinois Press, 1993), especially 271–272. For a more in-depth treatment of how lynching photographs became critical in the fight against lynching, see also Wood, *Lynching and Spectacle*, Chapters 6 and 7.

31   For a discussion of the impact that the Till murder case and more generally anti-black violence had on international perceptions of American democracy, see Mary Dudziak, *Cold War Civil Rights: Race and the Image of American Democracy* (Cambridge, MA: Harvard University Press, 2011), especially Chapter 1.

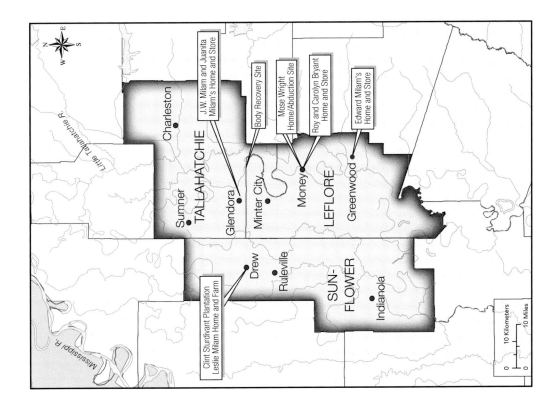

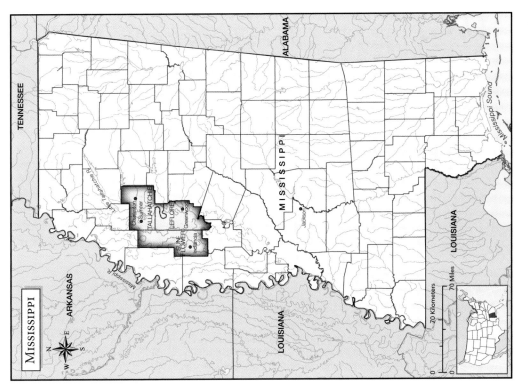

Map 3. Mississippi and Key Locations Associated with Emmett Till's Murder

that could link them to the murder. Most notably, they tried conceal Till's corpse by weighting it down with a cotton-gin fan and tossing it in the Tallahatchie River. They hoped Till's body would sink to the bottom of the river and would never be seen again. Their plan, of course, backfired: Till's body was found floating along the banks of the Tallahatchie River three days after the kidnapping. Moreover, after J. W. Milam and Roy Bryant kidnapped Till, Mose Wright reported the abduction to the Leflore County sheriff. With that information, the sheriff arrested Roy Bryant for kidnapping, and shortly thereafter J. W. Milam turned himself in.

Even though Till's killing does not fit the typical parameters of a lynching, he is mostly remembered as a lynching victim due to the widely disseminated photos of his bludgeoned face. Historians (myself included) often categorize Till's killing as a lynching (or use "lynching" and "murder" interchangeably to describe it) because referring to it as a murder seems woefully inadequate given the brutality visited upon him. With that said, murder—rather than lynching—is the most precise description of Till's killing. Admittedly there are differing definitions of what constitutes a lynching.[32] However, what most definitions of lynching share is an emphasis on lynching as an extralegal public killing organized by private citizens and witnessed by a group of people. In contrast, Milam, Bryant, and their accomplices attempted to conceal Till's murder and their identities, whereas lynch mobs and those who witnessed their handiwork wanted their identities to be known rather than concealed. This is evidenced by white spectators and mob participants who waited patiently and happily to pose for lynching photos.[33] In the final analysis, other historians and I find it useful to frame Till as a lynching victim because it suggests how his killing is a part of a long history of white supremacist violence.

TILL'S OPEN-CASKET FUNERAL

Upon the discovery of a corpse floating in the Tallahatchie River, Tallahatchie County sheriff Clarence Strider summoned Mose Wright to identify the body. Till was so badly beaten that Wright initially struggled

---

32   For the best explanation of the difficulties of defining lynching as well as how defining lynching created fissures within the antilynching movement, see Christopher Waldrop, "War of Words: The Controversy Over the Definition of Lynching, 1899–1940," *Journal of Southern History* 66, no. 1 (2000): 75–100.

33   For an overview and interpretation of lynching photography, see Dora Apel and Shawn Michelle Smith, *Lynching Photographs* (Berkeley: University of California Press, 2008). Additionally, see Dora Apel, *Imagery of Lynching: Black Men, White Women, and the Mob* (New Brunswick, NJ: Rutgers University Press, 2004).

to identify the body but ultimately was able to do so because Emmett was wearing a ring with initials "L.T." that had been given to him by his late father, Louis Till. After Wright identified the corpse, Sheriff Strider ordered Wright to immediately bury the body. As burial preparations were under way, Mamie Till was alerted, and she frantically contacted Chicago authorities, who intervened on her behalf to prevent the burial in Mississippi. Two days later, and approximately one week after his original departure, Till's lynched black body was returned to Chicago.[34]

The corpse was transported by train to Chicago and upon arrival was taken to the A. A. Raynor funeral home. Per Mississippi authorities' deal to release the body, his casket was not to be opened. However, when the corpse arrived at the funeral home, Mamie Till demanded that she be able to view the body. Initially, the mortician refused to open the casket but relented after Mamie Till insisted. The mortician briefly sent her away so that he might open the casket and assess the condition of the body. When she returned to the mortuary, the corpse had been removed from the casket and placed upon a table. With a few family members standing by, Mamie Till calmly and carefully surveyed the corpse in an effort to assuage any doubt that the body was in fact that of her son. Horrified by the brutality inflicted on him, Mamie Till decided that she did not want the mortician to improve his appearance for the funeral; rather, she wanted "the world to see what they did to my boy." She decided that the body would not be "touched up" and, in defiance of Mississippi authorities, his casket would be open for public viewing.[35]

Over the next five days, tens of thousands of mourners, and likely some curiosity seekers, viewed Till's body. Those who came to pay their respects were likely unprepared to see a fourteen-year-old youth whose face had been beaten beyond recognition. To underscore the savagery of her son's murder, Mamie Till taped three photos of him to the side of the casket. Stunned by what they saw, many onlookers wept, fainted, or both. The striking and unsettling sight of his disfigured face made manifest the depravity of Southern anti-black racism and the excesses of white supremacist violence. In the days following the funeral, black news outlets published photographs of Emmett Till's open-casket funeral. The publication of photos, specifically the photos of his disfigured face, provoked an immediate national and international condemnation of Mississippi as well as demands to bring his killers to justice.[36]

34 Anderson, *Emmett Till*, 45–52.

35 Ibid., 54–56.

36 Ibid.

THE TILL MURDER TRIAL AND JIM CROW JUSTICE

For many reasons, the Till murder trial was an extraordinary event. First and foremost, Southern courts and in particular county prosecutors were notorious for either ignoring or simply refusing to take seriously crimes perpetrated against blacks. One popular saying went "If a ni**er kills a white man, that's murder. If a white man kills a ni**er, that's justifiable homicide. If a ni**er kills another ni**er, well, that's one less ni**er."[37] So deeply entrenched was the idea that black people did not deserve equal justice that white Southerners asserted that there was one legal system for whites and one for blacks. For instance, laws selectively enforced against black people were referred to as "negro law."[38] For black defendants, "negro law" dictated that crimes committed against other black people were often ignored or only lightly punished by Southern courts. However, for crimes committed against white people, black defendants could expect to be sentenced to many years on the chain gang or worse. Given the culture of ignoring crimes perpetrated against blacks, it is likely that Mississippi authorities would not have prosecuted J. W. Milam and Roy Bryant had not Mamie Till brought national and international attention to Emmett Till's murder by having an open-casket funeral and allowing "the world to see what they did to my boy." Most importantly, Mamie Till's decision to allow newspapers to photograph and distribute pictures of Emmett Till's body made it the first *cause célèbre* of the civil rights era.[39]

The national and international attention that the Till case generated forced Mississippi authorities to take action; however, the case's heightened exposure did not alter how the segregated Mississippi criminal justice system operated. During the Jim Crow era (1880s to 1965), black Mississippians and black Southerners more generally were systematically excluded from serving on juries or practicing law. On rare occasions, Southern judges would allow black attorneys to represent a black defendant, but black attorneys were often forced to conduct their examination of witnesses from the back of the courtroom, where black spectators had to sit. Southern courts were so obsessed with imposing white supremacy that black Southerners who took the stand to testify were given a different Bible upon which to take their oath.[40]

---

37   Litwack, *Trouble in Mind*, 260 and 264.

38   Ibid., 258.

39   Jacqueline Goldsby, "The High and Low Tech of It: The Meaning of Lynching and the Death of Emmett Till," *Yale Journal of Criticism* 9 (1996): 249–261.

40   Litwack, *Trouble in Mind*, 328–358.

The Till murder trial resembled a typical Southern trial. For instance, the Leflore County Sheriff's Department (tasked with investigating the murder) was all white, the presiding judge was a white man, the lawyers for both the prosecution and defense were white men, and the jurors were all white and all male. In other words, black Mississippians would have little direct influence over the outcome of the trial. However, even though the trial took place in a segregated legal system, black witnesses were allowed to testify against white defendants, in contrast to typical Mississippi trials, due to the intense media attention the trial received and the presiding judge's desire for the trial to appear fair and impartial.

For a case that had such profound historical ramifications, the trial lasted only five days. The first day and a half were devoted to jury selection and the remaining three and a half days to the examination and cross-examination of witnesses. Five black witnesses (including Mamie Till) took the stand and offered testimony that supported the narrative that J. W. Milam and Roy Bryant had kidnapped and murdered Emmett Till. The number of black people taking the stand and directly implicating a white person in a crime as well as challenging white testimony was likely a record in Mississippi judicial history in 1955. The pivotal moment in the trial came when Mose Wright courageously took the stand and identified both Milam and Bryant as the men who kidnapped Till. Wright's testimony was courageous because often white Southerners intimidated or threatened blacks who dared to testify against whites. In fact, it was common for blacks who testified against whites to be subsequently beaten, murdered, or go missing.[41] For this reason, Wright and his family packed their belongings and left Mississippi soon after the trial.

During the trial, Milam and Bryant did not take the stand in their defense. Given that both men had admitted that they had kidnapped Till, taking the witness stand and undergoing a cross-examination would have only highlighted the fact that they did not and could not prove that they had returned Till to Wright's home as they contended. In their absence, Carolyn Bryant took the stand and offered testimony on how Till was a "ni**er man" who made lewd comments to her and grabbed her by the arm and waist during his visit to her store.[42] Her repeated reference to

41   Ibid., 253.

42   Carolyn Bryant testimony, *State of Mississippi vs. J. W. Milam and Roy Bryant, In the Circuit Court Second District of Tallahatchie County, Seventeenth Judicial District, State of Mississippi*, September Term, 1955, 269–270. During its two-year-long investigation (2004–2006) into Till's murder, the FBI recovered the long-lost Till murder trial transcript. The nearly complete transcript (missing only one page) provides an indispensable historical record of the case. For access to the full trial transcript, see "FBI: The Vault (Emmett Till: Part 1 and 2," FBI, https://vault.fbi.gov/Emmett%20Till%20.

the fourteen-year-old as a "man" was a strategic rhetorical choice meant to make palpable her insinuations that he intended to rape her. The presiding judge deemed her testimony tangential to the proceedings of the trial but nonetheless allowed her to offer testimony without the jury present. Carolyn Bryant's claim that Till had talked and behaved "ugly" played into white stereotypes about black men as sexual predators, which in turn created an emotional defense for why her husband and Milam would have been justified in kidnapping and murdering him. In other words, her testimony served to remind whites what the trial was really about—a white husband and his half-brother defending the honor and dignity of white Southern womanhood.

On the fifth and final day of the trial, the all-white and all-male jury deliberated. After approximately one hour, the jury delivered a not guilty verdict. Afterwards, a member of the jury bragged that it would not have taken that long had they not been told to "make it look good."[43] Mamie Till and her supporters were not present in the courtroom when the verdict was delivered. She had rightly surmised that the all-white jury would never render a guilty verdict against two white men for the murder of a black boy. Two months later, an all-white and all-male Tallahatchie Country grand jury opted not to indict Bryant and Milam for kidnapping Till despite the fact that both men admitted to doing so when they were initially arrested. The grand jury's rationale for not indicting on kidnapping charges is unknown, but it is safe to surmise that even had Milam and Bryant been indicted on kidnapping charges, they would not have been convicted.[44]

The exoneration of Bryant and Milam for Till's murder sent shock waves through America and the world. Two days following the verdict, large protest rallies occurred in New York, Chicago, and Detroit. In New York City, Mamie Till spoke to an estimated sixteen thousand people. With the trial now behind her, she painstakingly recounted how Mississippi whites had repeatedly referred to her as a "ni**er" and explained how the murder trial had been a farce and travesty of justice. Northern newspapers and particularly black newspapers castigated the verdict as a product of Mississippi's Jim Crow justice. Additionally, newspapers in Africa, Europe, and especially France criticized the verdict as shameful. Not satisfied with simply criticizing the verdict, black leaders and black civil rights organizations such as the NAACP and the Brotherhood of Sleeping Car Porters called for a federal investigation into the murder.[45] Even though Milam and Bryant

---

43 Tyson, *Blood of Emmett Till*, 179.

44 Anderson, *Emmett Till*, 153–155; 205–207.

45 Ibid., 168.

could not be tried for the same crime per double jeopardy statute in the U.S. Constitution, black activists believed there might be federal criminal charges on which Milam and Bryant could be indicted. Bringing a federal criminal indictment against Milam and Bryant and therefore removing the case from Mississippi's segregated judicial system was believed to be the best chance of holding the pair accountable for Till's murder. Despite black activists' calls for a federal investigation, the Federal Bureau of Investigation (FBI) refused to open a formal investigation into the murder because they maintained they had no jurisdiction—that is, there was no evidence to suggest that the murder involved crossing state lines, which could have triggered federal involvement in the case.[46] While Milam and Bryant's acquittal on murder charges and the grand jury's refusal to bring indictments for kidnapping brought an end to the case, the murder continued to reverberate.

LOOK MAGAZINE AND "THE SHOCKING STORY OF AN APPROVED KILLING"

In January 1956, five months after the trial had ended, *Look* magazine published a highly sensationalized account of the murder that was entitled "The Shocking Story of An Approved Killing." To persuade J. W. Milam and Roy Bryant to talk, journalist William Bradford Huie had paid them and their attorneys approximately $4,000 (plus a percentage of royalties) in exchange for allowing him exclusive rights to sell their story.[47] While Milam and Bryant did divulge to Huie that they murdered Till, Huie's article was far from a truthful confession. Rather, it was a self-serving narrative of Till's murder calculated to obscure the involvement of other accomplices, to show Till as cocky and boastful about his relations with white women, and to present Milam and Bryant as noble defenders of segregation and the Southern way of life. For example, Huie quoted Till as angrily boasting, "You bastards, I'm not afraid of you. I'm as good as you are. I've 'had' white women. My grandmother was a white woman."[48] Till apparently bellowed these defiant remarks as Milam and Bryant repeatedly beat him over the head with pistols. According to

---

46   Ibid., 166–170.

47   Ibid., 230.

48   Quoted in Christopher Metress, ed., *The Lynching of Emmett Till: A Documentary Narrative* (Charlottesville: University of Virginia Press, 2002), 207.

Huie, in response to Till's incendiary statements, the exasperated Milam and Bryant decided the only thing left to do was kill him. Huie quoted Milam as stating,

> Well, what else could we do? He was hopeless. I'm no bully; I never hurt a ni**er in my life. I like ni**ers—in their place—I know how to work 'em. But I just decided it was time a few people got put on notice. As long as I live and can do anything about it, ni**ers gonna stay in their place. Ni**ers ain't gonna vote where I live. If they did, they'd control the government. They ain't gonna go to school with my kids. And when a ni**er gets close to mentioning sex with a white woman, he's tired of livin'. I'm likely to kill him. Me and my folks fought for this country, and we've got some rights. I stood there in that shed and listened to that ni**er throw that poison at me, and I just made up my mind. "Chicago boy," I said, "I'm tired of 'em sending your kind down here to stir up trouble. Goddamn you, I'm going to make an example of you—just so everybody can know how me and my folks stand."[49]

The article portrayed Milam and Bryant as not wanting to kill Till; in fact, they said, they would not have killed him save for his repeated provocations. In other words, Huie presented a blatantly fabricated narrative of the murder that ultimately posited Till's brazenness as the chief reason why he was killed. In the end, Huie's main goal was not to present a truthful account of the murder but rather to provide a "shocking story" that would in turn generate publicity and profit.

Unsurprisingly, the *Look* magazine story reignited calls for a new trial. However, due to the double jeopardy clause in the Constitution, Milam and Bryant could not be retried for the murder. To the deep dismay of Mamie Till, the Till family, and supporters, neither Milam nor Bryant was ever held accountable for Emmett Till's kidnapping or murder.

THE HISTORICAL AND CONTEMPORARY SIGNIFICANCE OF THE TILL MURDER

Till's lynched black body refuses to die. It lives on in a number of guises. Since Till's horrific murder in 1955, he has been memorialized perhaps more than any other lynching victim in American history. In *Emmett*

---

49   Ibid.

Till in Literary Memory and Imagination, authors Harriet Pollack and Christopher Metress observe that Till's story

> through its multiple tellings and retellings haunts American memory and imagination. That haunting surfaces in the narratives we tell and the realities we live. Whether we are remembering it in the pages of a recent magazine or watching it reenacted again in the dark back roads of East Texas, what happened to Emmett Till is a presence that shapes the way we view and talk about race in America, sometimes wounding us, sometimes urging us to heal.[50]

Pollack and Metress identify approximately 140 literary works, including novels, stories, poems, plays, songs, musical scores, and movie and television scripts, that are based upon or significantly reference Till's lynching.

Till's cultural staying power is undeniably linked to the unforgettable nature of his disfigured face, but more deeply it has been made possible by America's collective preference for imagery that portrays black people as hapless victims. In *Seeing Through Race*, Martin Berger compellingly concludes that "'iconic' photographs endlessly reproduced in the newspapers and magazines of the period [civil rights movement], and in the history books that followed, were selected from among the era's hundreds of thousands of image for a reason: they stuck to a restricted menu of narratives that performed reassuring symbolic work."[51] He continues, "Photographs illustrating white-on-black violence proved both visually compelling to whites and capable of nudging society toward racial reforms. In depicting whites in charge, the photographs allowed white viewers to feel secure, and therefore more amenable to change, and in illustrating blacks as victims, they encouraged white sympathy for blacks, and hence more support for legislative action."[52] Given that Till's iconic open-casket photos can be thought of as founding images of the civil rights movement, it is reasonable to suggest that they perform the same work as do images of civil rights workers being attacked by enraged whites.

In recent years, Mamie Till's death in January 2003 reignited discussion of her and her son's legacy. Undoubtedly, she is best remembered for her selfless decision to allow her son's mutilated body to be viewed by the media. In preparing the body for public viewing, the mortician asked

---

50   Harriet Pollack and Christopher Metress, *Emmett Till in Literary Memory and Imagination* (Baton Rouge: Louisiana State University Press, 2008), 1.

51   Martin A. Berger, *Seeing Through Race: A Reinterpretation of Civil Rights Photography* (Berkeley: University of California Press, 2011), 6.

52   Ibid., 8.

Mamie Till if she would like his face to be touched up before the funeral, and she famously responded that she wanted the whole world to see what they did to her boy. In no small measure, this decision reflected the fact that "Till's body was not and could not be beautified."[53] Additionally, literature scholar Sandy Alexandre noted, "In airing her son's ugly death, [Mamie Till] Bradley ultimately shows that any attempt to aestheticize Till's body would have amounted to denying or forgetting the various ways in which that black body's relationship to southern spaces, particularly rural spaces, can literally transform that body."[54] In this spirit, *Jet* magazine published photos of Till's bludgeoned face in its September 1955 issue. Since the publication of the photos, Till's disfigured face has become the most recognizable lynching image in American history due in large part to Mamie Till's presenting her son's lynched black body to the world as a perfect victim of Southern racism.

Till's decision to publish photos of her son's corpse made the lynched black body a topic of world conversation. Historians tend to frame her decision and her active role in publishing images of her son's lynched black body as a courageous act. In fact, however, it was a subversive act because, historically, images of lynched black bodies were created and deployed by lynchers rather than the victims of lynching. In this way, Mamie Till disrupted the hegemony of the white-authored lynching archive and interrupted the white supremacist gaze that until this point largely dominated lynching narratives. In doing so, she made sure that the whole world would see what they did to her son and guaranteed that the world would never be able to forget her son's death the way that countless other black lynching victims were forgotten. Till's disfigured face told the story of white supremacy in a way that ten thousand treatises on the topic could not because the spectacle of his lynched black body made it impossible to look away.

Till's disfigured face framed for black and white Americans the horrors of unchecked racism and the foolhardiness of believing that segregation (and its close companion, racial violence) would come to an end "with all deliberate speed." More poignantly, literary historian Jacqueline Goldsby reflected, "Of the thousands of African Americans who were the victims of 'low-tech' lynchings, Till is the one people seem to remember most. For a generation of Americans—black and white alike—the memory of the teenager's murder was (and still is) a horrific souvenir that all was not right during the Eisenhower fifties, that violence lurked close to the surface of the era's

---

53   Sandy Alexandre, *The Properties of Violence: Claims to Ownership in Representations of Lynching* (Jackson: University of Mississippi Press, 2012), 148.

54   Ibid.,154.

consuming charm."[55] In other words, Till's lynched black body became a timeless symbol of lynching and black victimization because his youthful innocence suggested the innocence of all victims of vigilante violence. After all, for all his mother's warnings, Till had not been baptized in the fire of the South's racial etiquette, and therefore his wolf whistle to Carolyn Bryant that provoked his murder could be understood as an ill-advised but harmless transgression. Thus, Till's murder and the national media's subsequent framing of him as a perfect victim of white racism dislodged the black beast rapist discourse that had inspired Till's murder in the first place. Yet, by positioning Till's lynching as analogous to all other lynchings of black men, it compressed the history of white-on-black lynching into an easily consumable tale.

Nonetheless, Mamie Till's choice of an open-casket funeral attended by national and world media outlets necessitated an accounting for Till's death. The acquittal of Till's murderers in September 1955 simply postponed the accounting to another day. In fact, amidst the passing of Mamie Till in 2003, documentarians were seeking to uncover "the untold history" of Till's murder. Specifically, Stanley Nelson's *The Murder of Emmett Till* (2003) and Keith Beauchamp's *The Untold Story of Emmett Louis Till* (2005) identified accomplices (some of whom were alive at the time) to the kidnapping and murder. Nelson and Beauchamp's films challenged the widely held narrative that Milam and Bryant were the lone offenders. Since both were dead and their guilt had been established by their own admission in the 1956 *Look* magazine article, Beauchamp believed that a measure of justice for Till could be gained by prosecuting any surviving accomplices. Beauchamp's fascination with the murder began when, at ten years old, he came across a copy of *Jet* magazine's photo of Till's emaciated corpse. Beauchamp recalled that Till's disfigured face stuck with him in part because he was about the same age as Till when he saw the photo and because, before he would leave his home, his parents would often warn him, "Don't let what happened to Emmett Till happen to you."[56] For these reasons, Beauchamp asserted, "Emmett Till is deeply embedded in the African American community, especially the psyche of the black man."[57]

Others joined the growing chorus calling for reopening the Till case. Based on the Beauchamp and Nelson films and the exposure they received, pressure mounted from Till's family, the NAACP, the U.S. Congress, and various other entities to reopen the Till investigation. In May 2004, the FBI

---

55 Goldsby, "The High and Low Tech of It," 247.

56 Robin Finn, "Bringing History to Life, and a Crime to Light," *New York Times*, May 21, 2004.

57 Lynne Duke, "Specter of a Mississippi Murder; Nearly 50 Years After His Savage Death, Emmett Till Is a Potent Symbol," *Washington Post*, November 30, 2002.

announced that it would reopen the investigation to assess whether any new information could be ascertained that might aid new prosecutions.[58]

The FBI's announcement ignited a torrent of commentary concerning the appropriateness and significance of its renewed investigation. Opinions were diverse but mostly adhered to two positions. Those who supported reopening the case asserted that a measure of belated justice or at the least closure might occur if previously unknown accomplices in the murder were brought to justice. Assistant Attorney General R. Alexander Acosta said, "We owe it to Emmett Till, and we owe it to ourselves, to see whether after all these years some additional measure of justice remains possible."[59] NAACP President Kweisi Mfume declared, "This is a day of mixed emotions. We're glad that the investigation is being reopened but sad that it has taken so long. The nation can't put to bed this part of the civil rights era without resolving a glaring injustice such as this."[60] Others were not as hopeful. For them, while the FBI's efforts to reopen the case might reveal unknown accomplices and set the record straight, they believed that it could in no way bring about justice or a worthy closure to the case—the Till murder would remain an open wound. Black journalist Earl Ofari Hutchinson reflected, "Only when state and federal officials prosecute all of the suspected killers of innocent blacks during that lawless period can the book be permanently closed on the South's hideous legacy of racial murders."[61]

To effectively renew the Till investigation, the FBI decided in June 2005 that Till's body would need to be exhumed. During the FBI's preliminary investigation, it was discovered that an autopsy had never been completed; therefore, to establish Till's identity for once and for all, his body had to be removed from its resting place.[62] Understandably, the Till family disliked disturbing his burial site but eventually capitulated in order to see the case move forward. Several months after the autopsy, the FBI announced that the body was Till's and that his corpse might provide clues to the identity

---

58   For a detailed account of the reopening of the Emmett Till murder case, see Anderson, *Emmett Till*, Chapter 11.

59   Jerry Seper, "Probe Reopened in 1995 Murder," *Washington Times*, May 10, 2004.

60   Kevin Johnson and Laura Parker, "Feds Reopen 1955 Racial Slaying Case," *USA Today*, May 11, 2004.

61   Editorial, "Till Case Recalls a Chapter in American History," *USA Today*, May 21, 2004. For a comprehensive overview and critical analysis of the reopening of the case, see Margaret M. Russell, "Reopening the Emmett Till Case: Lessons and Challenges for Critical Race Prejudice," *Fordham Law Review* 73 (2005): 2101–2132.

62   Gretchen Ruethling, "After 50 Years, Emmett Till's Body Is Exhumed," *New York Times*, June 2, 2005.

of the alleged accomplices. In the end, however, physical evidence linking surviving accomplices to his murder was never discovered.

After months of investigative work, in March 2006, the FBI submitted an eight-thousand-page report to the Mississippi state authorities who would decide whether any of the new evidence warranted new prosecutions. After studying the FBI's investigative file, in February 2007, the district attorney for Mississippi's Fourth Judicial district (the district where the Till kidnapping occurred) impaneled a nineteen-member grand jury (composed of a near-equal number of black and white jurors) whose job it would be to determine whether there was sufficient evidence to indict Carolyn Bryant, who was alleged to have been present during Till's kidnapping. After listening to a detailed presentation of the evidence connecting her to the Till kidnapping and murder, the grand jury decided there was insufficient evidence to indict her for manslaughter.[63] Given that the grand jury was not asked to review evidence regarding other alleged accomplices, a jury trial for her role in the Till murder seemingly represented the last best chance for the Till family to hold someone accountable for the murder. In the end, no one has and presumably ever will be held accountable for the murder.[64] However, as a tribute to Emmett Till's life and death, President George W. Bush signed the Emmett Till Unsolved Civil Rights Crime Act into law in 2008, which has empowered the U.S. Department of Justice to reopen murder cases from the civil right movement era.[65]

Amid the FBI's investigation into the Till case and the criticism launched against the federal government for failing to take action with regards to lynching, Senate leaders mobilized to respond to criticism the Senate was receiving in the press in June 2005. Senate leaders felt compelled to do so because according to the press accounts, the Senate (particularly Southern senators) had blocked the passage of three antilynching bills that had been passed by the House of Representatives in 1922, 1937, and 1940. This admission was made all the more appalling when newspapers reported that despite Congress's failure to pass antilynching legislation to protect black Americans,

---

63   Anderson, *Emmett Till*, 337–340. Additionally, for a detailed overview of the FBI's investigation into the Till murder and the impaneling of a grand jury to review the FBI's investigative report, see Anderson, *Emmett Till*, Chapter 12.

64   In an 2008 interview with historian Timothy Tyson (which was extensively quoted in *The Blood of Emmett Till*), Carolyn Bryant revealed that Till did not physically accost her during their brief encounter. Following the publication of Tyson's book, the FBI reopened the Till case with Carolyn Bryant as the likely target of investigation. It is unclear what the FBI's objectives are in reopening the investigation, and to date no new charges have been brought against Carolyn Bryant.

65   Emmett Till Unsolved Civil Rights Crime Act of 2008, H.R. 923, 110th Congress, 1st session, http://www.judiciary.house.gov.

it paid nearly $500,000 to China, Italy, and Mexico on behalf of foreigners who were lynched in the United States.[66] Given the outcry for justice in the Till case, Senate leaders embraced its complicity in lynching and decided for the first time in American history to offer a formal apology for the poor treatment of black Americans. According to Senate Resolution 39, "The crime of lynching succeeded slavery as the ultimate expression of racism in the United States following Reconstruction" and as such the Senate "apologized to the victims of lynching and the descendants of those victims for the failure of the Senate to enact anti-lynching legislation." The resolution also stated, "The recent publication of 'Without Sanctuary: Lynching Photography in America' helped bring greater awareness and proper recognition of the victims of lynching."[67] In fact, Louisiana Senator Mary Landrieu and Virginia Senator George Allen, the architects of the Senate apology, revealed that James Allen's *Without Sanctuary* had laid bare for them the history of lynching and had compelled them to speak out against it. They admitted that without *Without Sanctuary*'s stark images of dismembered black lynching victims, a push for an apology would have occurred much more slowly. Landrieu said, "The intensity and impact of the pictures tell a story . . . the written words failed to convey. It has been an extremely emotional, educational experience for me. And the more I learned, the more sure I became [about] the effort to pass this resolution."[68]

In passing the historic resolution, Landrieu and other senators hoped that it would mark the "final word on this piece of American history."[69] Observers were quick to disagree. Most prominently, journalist and historian Laura Wexler asserted that it was impossible for the Senate to fully apologize for lynching. Wexler argued,

> It is admirable that the Senate has honestly and publicly acknowledged its role in American lynching. But just as no one can ask for forgiveness for a sin he or she did not commit, the Senate cannot apologize for the real crime of lynching: the countless burnings, beheadings, mutilations, assassinations, and hangings that occurred on

---

66   Avis Thomas-Lester, "Repairing Senate's Record on Lynching: Long Overdue Apology Would Be Congress's First for Treatment of Blacks," *Washington Post*, June 11, 2005.

67   Senate Resolution 39, 109th Congress, 1st session, http://www.govtrack.org.

68   Thomas-Lester, "Repairing Senate's Record." For a compelling argument about the shortfalls of the Emmett Till Unsolved Civil Rights Crime Act, see Barbara A. Schwabauer, "The Emmett Till Unsolved Civil Rights Act: The Cold Case of Racism in the Criminal Justice System," *Ohio State Law Journal* 71 (2010): 653–698.

69   Brian Debose, "Senate Regrets Lynching Inaction," *Washington Times*, June 12, 2005.

American soil. And it cannot apologize for the failure of countless juries to convict those who committed such hideous acts. Instead of providing comfort, it [the Senate] has pointed to the gaping hole that exists, and will always exist, where the other apologies—the ones from citizens—should have been.[70]

Wexler's commentary points to how lynchings and the history of federal and state inaction will remain an open wound in American life because the authentic apologies necessary for atonement are forever lost to history. As cultural heirs of the history of lynching, Wexler reminds contemporaries that our role, in fact our burden and charge, is to remember the history of lynching authentically. Remembering authentically means recognizing how American institutions such as the Senate not only encouraged, aided, and abetted Till's murder by their inaction. Remembering authentically means actively confronting past legacies as well as the present-day realities of racial violence in America. By remembering authentically in these ways, then and only then can we inch toward putting Till's lynched black body to rest.

---

70   Laura Wexler, "A Sorry History: Why an Apology From the Senate Can't Make Amends," *Washington Post*, June 19, 2005.

PART III
THE DOCUMENTS

DOCUMENTS OVERVIEW

In 1955, the Leflore and Tallahatchie County Police Departments did not conduct a thorough investigation of the Emmett Till murder. In fact, it was only with the assistance of local activists that key prosecution witnesses were identified and brought forth to testify at the trial. The first thorough investigation into Till's death came in 2004 when the FBI reopened the case. During the FBI's investigation, they recovered a long-lost trial transcript that offers first-person testimonies or accounts of the kidnapping and murder.

First-person accounts, along with other primary sources, are invaluable for historians attempting to construct a historical narrative. While trial transcripts offer important information, there are some challenges as well. First and foremost, to use trial transcripts appropriately, historians must understand the context in which they were created. For instance, a trial is an adversarial setting in which prosecution and defense attorneys attempt to convince a jury of a particular narrative of events while simultaneously attempting to undermine the narrative presented by the other side. Because defense and prosecution lawyers are not making arguments within a vacuum but rather to a jury of twelve people, it is important to understand the composition of the jury and the values of the jury members in order to put into context the narratives that the prosecution and defense advance during a trial. Only after understanding the rhetorical context in which a source is produced can a historian determine whether the information is credible.

I relied heavily on the recovered trial transcript to create the graphic history. Of particular importance was the direct testimony provided by Mose Wright, Willie Reed, Mamie Till, Carolyn Bryant, and Sheriff Clarence Strider. Because of their overall importance to the narrative, excerpted portions of Carolyn Bryant's and Mamie Till's direct testimony are included here (Documents 11 and 12). Beyond providing important information about the events that led to Till's kidnapping and murder, Carolyn Bryant's and Mamie Till's testimonies will help the reader understand how Till's identity/character played a crucial role in the trial and specifically the prosecution and defense lawyers' differing portrayals of him.

Readers will notice that trial testimony from J. W. Milam or Roy Bryant is not included here. This is because they elected not to take the stand in their defense during the trial. However, six months after they were found not guilty of the murder, both men admitted to having kidnapped and murdered Till in William Bradford Huie's "The Shocking Story of An Approved Killing," published in the January 1956 issue of *Look* magazine. Albeit deeply problematic, the source is of interest because it provides a narrative explanation as to why Milam and Bryant killed Till. An excerpt of the account is included as Document 15.

In addition to the excerpts from the trial transcript and the sensationalized *Look* account, I've included representative newspaper coverage (national/local as well as black press/white press) of Till's open-casket funeral, the murder trial, and post-trial commentary (Documents 4 through 10 and 13 through 16). Because photos of Till were crucial to telling the story of the murder and especially Southern racism, two photos of the open-casket funeral/burial as well a photo of Till taken shortly before he was killed are reproduced as Documents 1, 2, and 3. Taken together, the selection of primary sources should help students grasp the shifting and competing narratives about the meaning of the murder and what those narratives tell us about the Jim Crow South and American society more broadly in the 1950s.

DOCUMENT 1: PHOTO OF EMMETT TILL

AP Photo/Family Photo, Invision, Paul A. Hebert

Figure 1. Emmett Till poses in front of the family television on December 27, 1954.

DOCUMENT 2: PHOTO OF EMMETT TILL'S OPEN CASKET

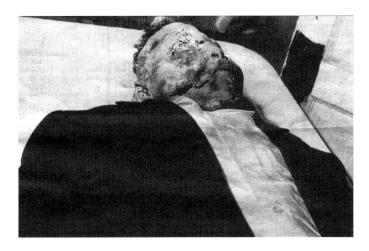

Figure 2. Emmett Till as he appeared at the funeral. Photos of Till's open casket appeared in the *Chicago Defender*, *Jet* magazine, and other black newspapers and magazines. Courtesy of *Chicago Defender*

DOCUMENT 3: PHOTO OF MAMIE TILL AT EMMETT TILL'S BURIAL

Figure 3. Mamie Till's reaction to the burial of her son Emmett Till. Bettman/Getty Images

DOCUMENT 4: TWO WHITE MEN CHARGED WITH KIDNAPPING NEGRO

DELTA DEMOCRAT-TIMES, AUGUST 30, 1955

Greenwood, Miss. (UP)—Two white men charged with kidnapping a 15-year-old Chicago Negro because they claimed he insulted the wife of one of the men claimed today they released the missing boy unharmed.

Sheriff George Smith and Roy Bryant, a storekeeper in nearby Money community and his half-brother, J.W. Nilan [Milam], were held on kidnap charges in the mysterious disappearance of Emmett Till of Chicago. They were arrested yesterday.

Smith said Till's whereabouts was the "$64 question."

Smith said he planned to question Bryant's wife, allegedly insulted by Till in Bryant's small store Saturday. He said there was "nothing new" to indicate where the boy might be.

It was possible that relatives of Till were hiding him out of fear for the youth's safety, Smith said, or had sent him back to Chicago. He said he "couldn't say" if the boy had been harmed.

The Bryants were said to have become offended when young Till waved to the woman and said "goodbye" when he left the store.

Witnesses said Mrs. Bryant identified the boy as "the one." The group then drove away with him. Smith and Bryant and Mila[m] claimed that later they found out he was not "the one" who allegedly insulted Mrs. Bryant, and that Till then was released.

Several Negro youths, all under 16, were reported to have been with Till in the store and were said to have forced him to leave the store for being "rowdy."

DOCUMENT 5: MUDDY RIVER GIVES UP BODY OF BRUTALLY SLAIN NEGRO BOY

MEMPHIS COMMERCIAL APPEAL, SEPTEMBER 1, 1955

Greenwood, Miss. Aug. 31—The body of a 14-year-old Negro boy was found in the muddy Tallahatchie River Wednesday and officers said two white men will be charged with his death.

A fisherman found the body of Emmett L. Till, who reportedly made "insulting remarks" to the wife of a Money, Miss., storekeeper. The body was weighted down with a heavy gin fan. He had been battered about the head and had a bullet wound above his right ear.

Sheriff H. C. Strider of Tallahatchie County said two men, jailed here on kidnap charges in the case since Monday, will be charged with murder Thursday.

Jurisdiction in the case will apparently be given to Tallahatchie County since the body was found in that county about 25 miles north of Greenwood. Tallahatchie County is directly north of Leflore County.

Held in Leflore County jail here are Roy Bryant, 29, whose wife was reportedly insulted by the youth, and his half-brother, J. W. Milam, about 40.

Orders were issued Wednesday night to arrest an unidentified third person for investigation in the case.

Sheriff Strider said the men would probably be kept in the jail here until the grand jury convenes Monday in Tallahatchie County.

However, Dist. Atty Stanny Sanders of Indianola said a more intensive investigation will be made to determine jurisdiction. He said the Negro's body was unclothed when it was found and he was known to be wearing shoes and white pants when he was abducted.

If the clothing can be found, its location would give an indication of where the slaying took place, Mr. Sanders said.

Sheriff Strider said he believed the boy was dumped into the river "about two days ago." He said Till's body was found "a good 10 miles" in Tallahatchie County, indicating the body was dumped into the river in that county since "it couldn't have floated up the river."

SAYS BOY WASN'T HURT

Earlier, Bryant told officers he took Till from the home of Till's uncle, Mose Wright, early Sunday. Bryant said, however, Till was released unharmed when it was found he wasn't the boy who insulted Mrs. Bryant, Leflore County Sheriff George Smith said.

Sheriff Smith and his deputies had been searching the Tallahatchie River, which flows by Money, since Monday.

The boy['s] uncle made the identification Wednesday, officers said.

Sheriff Strider said the body was found 12 miles north of Money by 17-year-old Floyd [Robert] Hodges who was running a trotline. "He went into the river in a motorboat and saw Till's feet and legs sticking up. He came back and called me. We went down and found the body hung in a drift," the sheriff said.

Officers reported the body had been weighted down with a cotton gin fan weighing about 125 pounds which was tied with barbed wire.

Officers said the youth had apparently been brutally beaten before he was shot. One officer said the beating was the "worst I've seen" in eight years of law enforcement.

Mamie Bradley, mother of the victim, said in Chicago she would seek legal aid to help convict the slayers of her son. His body will be returned to Chicago.

"The state of Mississippi will have to pay for this," she said. "I don't understand it. No matter what the boy did it wasn't worth killing him. I would expect that down there if the boy did something wrong he might come back to me beaten up. But they didn't even give me that," she sobbed.

REGRET IS VOICED

A statement issued by the head of Mississippi's pro-segregation Citizens Councils called the youth's death "regrettable."

Robert Patterson, executive secretary of the Citizens Councils, said at Winona the slaying could not be attributed in any way to activities of pro-segregation groups.

"This is a very regrettable incident," Mr. Patterson declared. "One of the primary reasons for our organization is to prevent acts of violence. We are doing our best in spite of constant agitation and inflammatory statements by the National Association for the Advancement of Colored People and outside agitators."

Gov. Hugh White said in Jackson he had not been officially notified of the recovery of the boy's body. He declined to comment on the case otherwise.

NAACP FIRES BLAST

In New York, Roy Wilkins, executive secretary of the NAACP, termed the slaying a "lynching" and charged that "it would appear that the State of Mississippi has decided to maintain white supremacy by murdering children."

Tuskegee Institute in Alabama said it had not received a report on the death and therefore had not classified it as [a] "lynching" or placed it in any other category.

Wilkins also leveled criticism at Governor White, saying, "We have protested to Governor White, but judging by past actions of the state Chief Executive, little action can be expected."

DOCUMENT 6: DESIGNED TO INFLAME

JACKSON DAILY NEWS, SEPTEMBER 2, 1955

I

On August 16 of 1954, a New York City Negro factory worker, Willard Menter, awakened from a drunken stupor on a park bench in Brooklyn near the East River. The pain that awakened him was caused by lighted cigarettes being pressed against the naked sole of his foot.

When he roused himself enough to comprehend that there were four dark figures standing over him, he started to run. The four figures halted him, beat him mercilessly and then walked him to the East River, where he was pushed in, senseless. His body was found some time later.

A passerby had seen something of what took place and alerted Brooklyn Police, who, an hour later, arrested four youths for the murder of the Negro worker. The four confessed to not only that killing but also to the brutal slaying of steeple jack Reinhold Ulrickson. More, they admitted horsewhipping several girls and sadistically burning the legs of another man.

Everyone agreed that the murder of Menter was a frightful crime and everyone rallied to deplore the fact that the teen-aged boys who committed the crime had no cause for their action. The boys were subsequently sentenced to long terms in the New York State penitentiary.

No one called the killings anything other than useless, senseless acts of savagery. No one believed they were lynchings. NAACP Executive President Roy Wilkins admitted Thursday that his organization did not classify the murder as lynching but said he did not know why. The National Association for the Advancement of Colored People didn't turn a hand about Willard Menter's death. The courts of New York took care of that matter.

II

Tuskegee Institute, which seems to have the official task of classifying lynchings, says that a lynching is a race killing in which three or more persons take part. Tuskegee Institute did not classify the New York murder as a lynching in spite of the fact that the four boys who murdered the Negro man were all white.

III

Last Sunday, a teen-aged Negro boy, Emmitt [Emmett] Louis Till, was kidnapped and murdered by what the Leflore County sheriff says witnesses say were two white men and a white woman. The boy was a visitor to the little Mississippi community of Money. He is said to have given a "wolf whistle" at the wife of storekeeper Roy Bryant. The boy was a polio victim and seems to have had a speech impediment which might have caused the whistle. He was also said to have been "feeble minded."

His body was found in the Tallahatchie River, weighted with a gin fan, a bullet behind one ear and his face badly torn by what must have been a savage beating.

At once, Sheriff George Smith, of Leflore County, arrested the storekeeper, Roy Bryant, and his half-brother, J. W. Milam. Both men were said by the sheriff to have been identified as being in the automobile which drove the Negro boy from the home of his uncle, whom he was visiting.

Sheriff Smith said the two men denied killing the boy and had instead released him at once.

Sheriff Smith took exactly the same action as the Brooklyn Police Department after being notified of the crime. He did his sworn duty, as any law enforcement officer is expected to do.

IV

Gov. Hugh White has ordered district attorneys from two countries to investigate the crime. The governor said Mississippi "will not tolerate" such actions. He is right.

Every responsible citizen in the state of Mississippi agrees that the murder was a brutal, senseless crime and just incidentally, one which merits not one iota of sympathy for the killers. The people of Mississippi deplored this evil act just as much as the people of New York State deplored the terrible crime of the teen-agers.

Citizens Council officials have deplored the act. Robert Patterson, executive secretary, said a "primary reason" for the existence of his organization was to "prevent violence."

The kidnap-killing must have been the act of a depraved mind, or minds. The people of Money, where the crime took place, were shocked and appalled. Everyone is in solid agreement that it was a stupid, horrible crime. Intelligent Mississippians can only suppose it came about in the sick mind of men who should be removed from society by due course of law.

V

In New York City, NAACP's executive secretary, R[o]y Wilkins, callously called the killing a lynching. He said that "it would appear from this lynching that the State of Mississippi has decided to maintain white supremacy by murdering children. The killers of the boy felt free to lynch him because there is in the entire state no restraining influence of decency, not in the state capital, among the daily newspapers, the clergy nor any segment of the so-called better citizens."

Just how he terms the murder a lynching when NAACP and Tuskegee Institute declined to label the New York City murder as a lynching is not made clear. What does come clear, by implication, is that anytime a Negro is murdered by whites in Mississippi, it will be considered a lynching by the NAACP. That is because the NAACP is trying its best to inflame the nation against the South in general and Mississippi in particular. It serves only to arouse hatred and fear.

Perhaps NAACP will try to hide behind the wording of a proposed Federal anti-lynching bill which declares that lynching must be an ["]act under pretext of services to justice, race or tradition." But there is no more evidence in this case to show racial hatred on the part of those who murdered the boy than there was to show racial hatred for the New York factory worker in the minds of the sadistic quartet of teen-agers.

Mississippi law officers are doing all they can to bring the guilty parties to justice. There is nothing but contempt in the hearts of all right-minded Mississippians for those who committed this evil crime.

But the kidnap-murder was not a lynching and when NAACP so says, it proves its cynical purpose of inflaming the Negro people of this state against the whites. Its reckless allegations must not go unchallenged.

DOCUMENT 7: MEDDLING IN LOCAL CASE CREATES PROBLEMS

GREENWOOD MORNING STAR, SEPTEMBER 6, 1955

The meddling of outside agitators in the Till murder case has created a number of ugly problems, and there is a growing resentment against those who seek to use the affair to create strife and ill feeling.

The Till case started out as a routine crime affair which the Leflore County officers were handling in the same manner they would a crime of one white against another or involving only negroes. They prosecuted the investigation of the case with commendable vigor and were making excellent progress when the mayor of Chicago, the NAACP and other outsiders tried to create a false impression by labeling it as an act of race hatred which whites in Miss. might condone.

Justice in the Till case appeared certain of being carried out by the court had the outsiders not interfered. Now there are rumors that the whole thing was a plant by the NAACP and sympathy is swinging to the side of the accused.

A dangerous situation has been created by the threats of certain persons that Northern negroes are coming to Miss. to interfere with the case. The National Guard patrolling the courthouse and streets is mute evidence of the jittery situation which exists, and which might erupt into a holocost [sic] which would claim the lives of innocent persons.

Greenwood has had a lot of unwarranted and unfavorable publicity which all our good citizens, both white and colored[,] regret very much.

This is a time for cool heads and calm action. There is no actual danger of an invasion of armed outsiders. All the reports of such have been explored and found to be utterly fantastic. We have checked the sale of firearms and shells the past few days and find that there has been a scare which is not only regrettable but dangerous. There are plenty of officers to take care of all situations and there is absolutely no danger or need for civilians to arm themselves. In fact, there is much greater danger from the possibility of gunshot accidents with weapons in the hands of those who are not experienced in their use than there is from race trouble.

The negro leaders of Leflore County are cooperative and anxious to clear the whole matter without trouble. They realize the problems which exist and are cooperating with the authorities in trying to keep agitators from causing trouble.

We sum up the whole thing by giving the warning that the agitation is inspired by Communists or by persons who have become unwitting victims of the Communist plan to stir up trouble where possible. The way to combat the situation is to handle this situation with cool heads and firm hands.

DOCUMENT 8: MOTHER'S TEARS GREET SON WHO DIED A MARTYR

MATTIE SMITH COLIN, *CHICAGO DEFENDER*, SEPTEMBER 10, 1955

"Oh, God. Oh, God. My only boy," Mrs. Mamie Bradley wailed as five men lifted a soiled paper-wrapped bundle from a huge brown wooden mid-victorian box at the Illinois Central Station in Chicago Friday and put it into a waiting hearse.

The bundle was the bruised and bullet-ridden body of little 14-year-old Emmett Louis Till of Chicago, who had been lynched down in Money[,] Miss.

Limp with grief and seated in a wheel chair among a huge throng of spectators, Mrs. Bradley cried out: "Lord you have your only son to remedy a condition, but who knows, but what the death of my only son might bring an end to lynching."

As Bishop Louis Ford and Rev. Isaac Roberts prayed and rolled the wheel chair, Mrs. Bradley screamed, "Let me pray," and assisted by the ministers dropped to her knees, crying, "Lord take my soul, show me what you want me to do and make me able to do it."

A morbid silence engulfed the station. Veteran newspapermen and photographers, whose daily schedules include murders and fatal accidents, were grim-faced as they watched the procedure and then went about their work.

Dr. T. R. M. Howard of Mound Bayou, Miss., while boarding a plane at Midway Airport here Wednesday said when queried about this case, "There is going to be hell to pay in Mississippi."

DOCUMENT 9: NATION SHOCKED, VOW ACTION IN LYNCHING OF CHICAGO YOUTH

CHICAGO DEFENDER, SEPTEMBER 10, 1955

Mrs. Mamie Bradley, of Chicago, declared: "The whole state of Mississippi is going to pay for this thing. He was a good boy. I know he didn't do anything to deserve that."

Till's body was found Wednesday in the Tallahatchie river by Floyd Hughes, 17, while fishing.

Leaders and government officials in Illinois and throughout the country deplored the ugly incident and called for immediate action.

The NAACP charged that Mississippi had decided to maintain white supremacy by killing children. Tuskegee Institute late last week was investigating the slaying to see if it can be officially classified as a lynching.

Mississippi had been free of lynchings since 1951 until last May.

Young Till is the third person to fall in Mississippi's "anti-Negro war" in less than five months.

The Rev. George W. Lee, 51, was blasted to death by unknown persons in Belzoni, Miss., and Lamar Smith, 63, was shot to death virtually on the court house steps in Brookhaven on Aug. 13. Both had been active in the voter registration drive.

The situation in Mississippi has been growing steadily worse since the Supreme Court outlawed segregation in public schools on May 17, 1954.

Whites in the state have organized themselves into groups known as the Citizens Councils and have attempted to effect an economic freeze in order to force Negroes to stop "agitating" for integration.

DOCUMENT 10: THOUSANDS AT RITES FOR TILL

ROBERT ELLIOTT, *CHICAGO DEFENDER*, SEPTEMBER 10, 1955

More than 50,000 people appeared to mourn over the body of 14-year-old Emmett Louis Till as it lay in state in the Rayner Funeral Home at 4141 Cottage Grove, on Friday.

Throughout the night the lines stretched a block long outside the home. The scene was duplicated as thousands attempted to get into funeral services at Chicago's Roberts Temple Church of God in Christ, 4021 S. State St. A public address system carried the service to the crowds standing in the streets Saturday.

Rev. Isiah Roberts officiated at the service. He called the burial lynching [sic] of the boy a black mark against the U.S. and called for justice and a swift trial of the boy's slayers.

BISHOP GIVES EULOGY

The eulogy was delivered by Bishop Louis Ford.

Officials of the funeral home where the angry, the awed and the curious filled in to view the remains of the boy, who may or may not have insulted a white woman, declared they had never seen anything like it.

Many of the people were in an angry mood, they said.

As the crowd grew larger, police assistance was needed to keep the line moving and the people under control.

The condition of the body did not help, said a Rayner spokesman. Efforts at reconstruction were hampered by the advanced decomposition of the body.

The boy was found three days after his body had been thrown into the Tallahatchie River. The marks of his barbed wire bindings were still visible.

The people saw them and grew angry.

Few of them had ever seen or heard of "Bo" Till until he whistled or made an ugly remark to a white woman in Mississippi and doomed himself.

Most of them were thinking it is no crime for a boy to whistle at a pretty woman. They were thinking, "My son might do it—or yours." And thinking that, they suddenly felt "Bo" Till belonged to them. And they came to see him. Many of them talked to him.

They all swore they'd never forget him.

DOCUMENT 11: EMMETT TILL MURDER TRIAL TRANSCRIPT, DIRECT AND CROSS EXAMINATION OF MAMIE TILL

MAMIE BRADLEY TESTIMONY, *STATE OF MISSISSIPPI VS. J. W. MILAM AND ROY BRYANT*, IN THE CIRCUIT COURT SECOND DISTRICT OF TALLAHATCHIE COUNTY, SEVENTEENTH JUDICIAL DISTRICT, STATE OF MISSISSIPPI, SEPTEMBER TERM, 1955, 183–212

A witness introduced for and on behalf of the State, being first duly sworn, upon her oath testified as follows:

DIRECT EXAMINATION

BY MR. SMITH[1]:

Q: Your name is Mamie Bradley?

A: Yes, Sir.

---

1   Robert Smith, one of the attorneys representing the prosecution team, led the direct examination of Mamie Till.

Q: Where do you live, Mamie?

A: Chicago, Illinois.

Q: Mamie, did you have a son who in his lifetime was known as Emmett Till?

A: Yes, Sir.

Q: How old was Emmett?

A: Fourteen years of age.

Q: Is his Father living today?

A: No, Sir. He died in the service.

Q: He died in the service?

A: Yes, Sir.

Q: Do you remember the date of his death?

A: Yes, Sir; the 2nd of July, 1945.

Q: Where was he when he died?

A: In the European Theatre.

Q: Mamie, in the first part of September, 1955, or the last part of August, were you advised that your son, Emmett Till, had been in some difficulty or trouble down here?

A: Yes, Sir.

Q: And who advised you of that?

A: The Mother of Curtis Jones, Mrs. Willa Mae Jones.

Q: And how did she advise you? Was it by telephone?

A: Yes, Sir.

Q: Where was your son at that time?

A: He was visiting my Uncle, Mose Wright, in Money, Mississippi.

Q: And when did he come down here?

A: He left Chicago, Illinois, on the 20th of August.

Q: And I believe he was supposed to come home shortly thereafter, is that right?

A: Yes, Sir. He was going to stay two weeks.

Q: Now, later, after you got that information, was a body sent to Chicago that was supposed to be the body of your son, Emmett Till?

A: Yes, Sir.

Q: And where was that body first seen by you?

A: At the A. A. Rayner Funeral Home.

Q: Did you observe the body there?

A: Yes, I did.

Q: And where was the body when you saw it there at the funeral home?

A: The first time I saw it, it was still in the casket.

Q: Did you see it later on?

A: Yes, Sir. I saw it later on after it was removed from the casket and placed on a slab.

Q: At the time it was still in the casket, had anything been done to the body then, if you know?

A: No, Sir. The seal had never been broken the first time I saw the body.

Q: When the body was placed on the slab, was anything done then? Had anything been done to the body after it was removed from the casket?

A: The only change was that the body had been clothed.

Q: It had some clothes on then?

A: Yes, Sir.

Q: Mamie, I wish you would state to the court and jury whether you could identify the body you saw there at the funeral home as that of your son, Emmett Till?

A: I positively identified the body in the casket and later on when it was on the slab as being that of my son, Emmett Louis Till.

Q: Will you please tell the court and jury how you looked at it and what you did in identifying it?

A: I looked at the face very carefully. I looked at the ears, and the forehead, and the hairline, and also the hair; and I looked at the nose and the lips, and the chin.

I just looked at it all over very thoroughly. And I was able to find out that it was my boy beyond a shadow of a doubt.

Q: Mamie, when your husband, the father of Emmett Till, was killed overseas, were his effects sent to you?

A: Yes, Sir. They were.

Q: I will ask you if in those effects there was a ring?

A: Yes, Sir. There was a ring.

Q: What kind of a ring was it? What color was it?

A: The ring was white or it looked like some kind of white metal.

MR. BRELAND: Now, Your Honor, we now object to the testimony of this witness with reference to the effects, or what is purported to be the effects of her dead husband being sent to her, without showing just who, when and how those effects were sent.

THE COURT: Yes, I believe there would have to be a prior connection on the identification of the ring, I think.

MR. SMITH: All we are trying to do, Your Honor, is to identify the ring that the boy had on.

MR. SMITH: Yes, Sir.

Q: Mamie, I will ask you if your son had a ring and frequently wore a ring that was sent along in the effects of your husband that you got?

A: Yes, Sir.

MR. BRELAND: We object to that, Your Honor, for the reason that she said that the effects were sent to her that were supposed to belong to her dead husband. But it hasn't been shown in evidence anything about the identity of those effects.

THE COURT: The objection is overruled.

Q: I now hand you a ring, Mamie, that has engraved on it "May 25, 1943", with the large initials "L.T.", and I ask you if that was among the effects that were sent to you which were purported to be the effects of your dead husband?

A: Yes, Sir.

Q: What was your husband's name?

A: Louis Till.

Q: In other words, his initials were "L.T."?

A: Yes, Sir.

Q: And after you got this ring along with his effects, what happened to it?

A: I kept the ring in a jewelry box, but it was much too large for the boy to wear. But since his twelfth birthday, he has worn it occasionally with the aid of scotch tape or string. He had to have something else on with it to make it fit his hand tightly enough. But usually though it was kept in his personal jewelry box. And on the morning of September—or of August 20th when he got ready to board the train, he was looking in his jewelry box to get some cuff links, I think it was, and when he looked in the box there, he saw this ring, and he put it on his hand, or on his finger, and he shook his hand, to make sure that it would stay on there and not fall off.

And I remember that I casually remarked to him I said, "Gee, you are getting to be quite a grown man." And then he said to me—

Q: Now don't tell what he said. But did he then put the ring on his finger?

A: Yes, Sir.

Q: And he left Chicago with it, did he?

A: Yes, Sir.

Q: And that was the ring he had when he came down here to Mississippi?

A: Yes, Sir.

Q: Now Mamie, I have here a picture which has been introduced in evidence as Exhibit 1 to the testimony of Mr. Strickland here in this trial. And I hand you that picture and ask you if that is a picture of your son, Emmett Till?

A: Yes, Sir.

Q: That is him, isn't it?

A: Yes, Sir.

MR. SMITH: If the Court please, just one minute—these pictures have never been shown to the jury, and I wonder at this point if you might let the jury look at them.

THE COURT: They can have them. They have been introduced in evidence. (The two exhibits, Exhibits 1 and 2 to the testimony of Mr. Strickland are given to the members of the jury for examination.)

MR. SMITH: You may take the witness.

CROSS EXAMINATION

BY MR. BRELAND[2]:

Q: Mamie, where were you born?

A: I was born in Webb, Mississippi.

Q: You were born in Webb, Mississippi?

A: Yes, Sir.

Q: That is a little town just two miles south of here, is that right?

A: I can't tell you the location.

Q: But it is about two miles south of Sumer, isn't it?

A: I don't know.

Q: When did you leave Mississippi?

A: At the age of two.

---

2   Jesse Breland, lead defense attorney for Roy Bryant and J. W. Milam, questioned Mamie Till during the cross examination.

Q: Then you have just been told that you were born in Webb, Mississippi? You don't remember, is that right?

A: Yes, Sir.

Q: What was your mother's name?

A: Alma Carthan.

Q: Was she born in Mississippi?

MR. CHATHAM: We are going to object to this, if Your Honor please. This is highly immaterial in this case, and I am sure we want to get through with this trial some time.

THE COURT: I think we are going a little far afield. But I will let the witness answer that question.

THE WITNESS: Yes, Sir.

Q: Do you remember who left with you when you left Mississippi?

MR. SMITH: We object to that, Your Honor. That has nothing to do with this case at all.

THE COURT: The objection is sustained.

Q: When you can first remember, where were you living?

A: In Argo, Illinois.

Q: How far is that from Chicago?

A: Approximately thirteen miles.

Q: And how long did you live there at Argo, Illinois?

MR. SMITH: If the Court please, we are going to object to this line of questioning. It is highly immaterial and has nothing at all to do with this case.

THE COURT: The objection is sustained.

Q: When did you move to Chicago?

MR. SMITH: We object to that, Your Honor.

THE COURT: The objection is sustained.

Q: What is your age, Mamie?

A: Thirty-three.

Q: When your son, Emmett, left home with the intention of coming to Mississippi, when was his mind made up to come to Mississippi?

A: One week previous to the day he left.

Q: Did you and him talk about it?

A: Yes, Sir.

Q: And you discussed it together between you, did you?

A: Yes, Sir.

Q: And how many times did you discuss it with him?

A: I probably wouldn't be able to tell you that.

Q: Well, about how many times?

A: Several times at least.

Q: Did you go with him to the train when he left Chicago?

A: Yes, Sir.

MR. SMITH: We object to that, Your Honor. That has nothing to do with this.

THE COURT: The objection is sustained.

Q: Mamie, did Emmett ever have any trouble up there in Chicago? Was he ever in any trouble up in Chicago?

A: No, Sir.

MR. SMITH: We object to that, Your Honor.

THE COURT: The object is sustained.

Q: By the way, did you have any insurance on Emmett Till?

A: Yes, Sir.

MR. SMITH: We object to that, Your Honor.

THE COURT: I am going to overrule your objection to that question.

Q: Did you have any life insurance on him?

A: Yes, Sir.

Q: How much did you have?

A: About four hundred dollars straight life.

Q: You had about four hundred dollars insurance on him?

A: I had a ten-cent policy and a fifteen-cent policy, two weekly policies, and they equaled four hundred dollars.

Q: You had two policies that equaled four hundred dollars?

A: Yes, Sir.

Q: How long had you had those policies out on him?

A: Almost from his birth.

Q: With what companies were they?

A: Well, Metropolitan—

MR. SMITH: We object to that, Your Honor.

THE COURT: The objection is sustained.

Q: To whom were those policies payable?

MR. SMITH: We object to that, Your Honor.

THE COURT: The object is overruled.

THE WITNESS: Will you repeat the question, please?

Q: To whom were those policies payable? Who was the beneficiary in those policies?

A: I was the beneficiary on one and my Mother was on the other.

Q: Were they both for four hundred dollars each?

A: Well, one was for a hundred and ninety-three dollars, I think, and one was a little bit more. It was approximately four hundred dollars on the two of them.

Q: And have you collected on those policies?

A: No, Sir.

Q: Have you tried to collect on them?

MR. SMITH: We object to that, Your Honor. That is highly irrelevant.

THE COURT: The objection is overruled.

Q: Have you tried to collect on those policies?

A: I have been waiting to receive a death certificate.

Q: Have you contacted the insurance companies about the policies?

A: Yes, Sir.

Q: And you and your mother, both, have done that?

A: Yes, Sir, together.

Q: Now, Mamie, what newspapers do you subscribe to in Chicago?

MR. SMITH: We object to that, Your Honor.

THE COURT: The objection is sustained.

Q: Do you read the CHICAGO DEFENDER?

MR. SMITH: We object to that, Your Honor.

THE COURT: The objection is sustained.

MR. BRELAND: Your Honor, I think this is important because I have some exhibits that I want the witness to identify.

MR. CHATHAM:[3] If the Court please, I think it is perfectly obvious what he is trying to get at. And I think counsel should be counseled not to ask any more questions like that.

THE COURT: The objection is sustained. Now, will you gentlemen of the jury step back in the jury room a moment, please.[4]

---

3   Gerald Chatham was Tallahatchie County District Attorney and one of the prosecuting attorneys during the Emmett Till murder trial.

4   At this point in the trial, Milam and Bryant's defense team sought to dispute the credibility of the prosecution's photos representing the likeness of Emmett Till. In order to insure the jury's opinion of the photos were not biased, the presiding judge decided the discussion of whether the photos could be entered as evidence would be discussed without the jury present.

(The jury retired to the jury room, and the proceeding continued in the absence of the jury.)

Q: Do you subscribe to the CHICAGO DEFENDER?

A: No, Sir, I don't subscribe to the paper, but I do buy it and read it.

Q: You buy it and read it?

MR. SMITH: If the Court please, we want the record to show that we object to all this line of questioning.

THE COURT: The jury is out of the room, and the Court has already sustained your objection.

Q: Have you been reading the CHICAGO DEFENDER since the trial of this case?

A: Yes, Sir.

Q: And also since the incident happened that has been referred to here?

A: Yes, Sir.

Q: And you have been getting it, have you?

A: Yes, Sir. I read it every week, anyway.

Q: And you read everything in it, do you?

A: I wouldn't say the entire thing.

Q: I mean, you read everything in it referring to this incident, do you?

A: No, Sir. I haven't read the paper all through since I found out the child had been found dead.

Q: Did you read the paper of Saturday, September 17th?

A: I would have to look at it to see.

Q: I will hand it to you, the paper of that edition. (A paper is shown to the witness.)

A: I haven't even seen this one, I don't think. This is the national. I might have seen the other one. You see, there are two DEFENDERS. But the national, I haven't seen.

Q: These papers are edited by colored people, is that right?

A: Yes, Sir.

Q: I will hand you a portion of that particular paper, that edition of that particular paper, and ask you to look at the photograph and see if you have seen that?

A: I have seen this picture but not in this paper. I saw a much smaller picture in another copy of the DEFENDER.

Q: But is that a likeness of the picture you did see?

A: Yes, Sir.

Q: Have you a photograph of your son, Emmett Till, with you?

A: Yes, Sir. I have.

Q: And have you got it on your person?

A: It is with my Father in the witness chambers.

Q: When was that photograph made?

A: Two days after Christmas, 1954.

Q: 1954?

A: Yes, Sir.

Q: Did you have several of those photographs made?

A: Yes, Sir.

Q: And did you furnish any of those photographs to members of the press?

A: Yes, Sir.

Q: And that was for photographic purposes to put in the papers, is that right?

A: Yes, Sir.

Q: Now I hand you a paper—this is not a Chicago paper; this is the MEMPHIS PRESS-SCIMITAR—and I will ask you to look at that photograph in the upper left part of the paper and state whether that is a copy of that photograph you furnished the press?

A: Yes, Sir. I have a copy of it with me if you would like to see it.

Q: And you don't have more than one photograph of that picture with you?

A: I have one copy of three different pictures.

Q: You have three different pictures with you?

A: Yes, Sir.

Q: Have you got any more of those at home?

A: Yes, Sir.

Q: In other words, you could use one copy here, and you wouldn't be deprived of anything by having one copy in the record? You would still have a copy for yourself?

A: Yes, Sir.

Q: And you could have more copies made of those if you wanted them, is that right?

A: Yes, Sir.

MR. BRELAND: If the Court please, we would like for those to be produced here at this particular hearing so that she might identify those photographs she might have with her.

MR. SMITH: We object to that, Your Honor.

THE COURT: Can you get the photographs?

THE WITNESS: Yes, Sir. My Father has them in the witness room.

MR. SMITH: What is your Father's name?

THE WITNESS: John Carthan. And he has the pictures with him. They are in this coat.

MR. BRELAND: Tell them to bring John Carthan to the courtroom and to bring his coat with him.

(After a short period, an envelope is produced and handed to the witness on the stand.)

Q: Mamie, will you take out those photographs that are in that envelope?

A: Yes, Sir. (Three photographs are given to Mr. Breland by the witness.)

Q: Mamie, you have presented to counsel for the defendants what purports to be three separate photographs of your son, one of which has a woman in it taken with him. Is that you?

A: Yes, Sir.

Q: Can you tell the court and jury the last one of the photographs made, if they were made at different times?

A: All of these pictures were made on the very same day.

Q: They were all made on the same day?

A: Yes, Sir. As a matter of fact, there was one more picture made at the time, and I believe it is one where a picture was taken where he was lying across the bed and looking this way, but unfortunately, I do not have one of those with me.

Q: Mamie, I hand you now what purports to be a photograph of some person. Will you state whose photograph that is?

A: That is a photograph of Emmett Louis Till.

Q: That is your son?

A: Yes, Sir.

MR. BRELAND: We would like to have that marked as an exhibit for identification, please.

THE COURT: All right.

(A photograph is marked as Exhibit 1 to the testimony of Mamie Bradley for identification by the reporter.)

Q: Mamie, I believe you stated that the photograph on the front page of that PRESS-SCIMITAR, in the upper-left-hand corner of those photographs, of the group of photographs there, that it is a photograph of your son?

A: Yes, Sir.

Q: Was that a picture that was made from one of the photographs that you have testified about?

A: Not one of these three that I have shown you.

Q: But it was one taken at the same time?

A: Yes, Sir.

MR. BRELAND: This is on the front page of the edition of the MEMPHIS PRESS-SCIMITAR of Thursday, September 15th, 1955; and we offer that photograph in the upper left-hand corner on that front page of that paper as Exhibit 2, for purposes of identification by this witness.

THE COURT: All right.

(A photograph is marked as Exhibit 2 to the testimony of Mamie Bradley for identification by the reporter.)

Q: Mamie, I hand you a paper, being page 19 of the CHICAGO DEFNEDER, on the date of September 17th, 1955, which purports to be a photograph of some person.

Will you look at that and state whether or not that is also a photograph of Emmett Till or the person who was shipped back to Chicago that you saw at funeral home there?

A: This is a picture of Emmett Louis Till as I saw it at the funeral home.

Q: This is a picture of the body as you saw it in the funeral home in Chicago, Illinois?

A: Yes, Sir.

Q: And being the picture of the same body which you then identified as Emmett Till?

A: Yes, Sir.

Q: And which you now identify as that of Emmett Till, is that right?

A: Yes, Sir.

MR. BRELAND: Now, if Your Honor please, we ask that this be marked as Exhibit 3 to the testimony of this witness for the purposes of identification.

THE COURT: All right.

(A photograph is marked as Exhibit 3 to the testimony of Mamie Bradley for identification by the reporter.)

Q: Mamie, do you state to the Court that the photographs which you now have identified as Exhibit 1 to your testimony for purposes of identification, and the photograph which you identified in the PRESS-SCIMITAR as Exhibit 2 to your testimony for purposes of identification, and the photograph in the CHICAGO DEFENDER, under date of September 17th, 1955, as Exhibit 3 to your testimony for purposes of identification, are a likeness of those photographs of those scenes? And do you state that they are true pictures of the scenes you saw?

A: Yes, Sir.

THE COURT: Have you finished with your examinations?

MR. BRELAND: I believe we have, Your Honor. And we submit that these are proper at this time.

THE COURT: Have you finished with your examination of this witness outside the hearing of the jury?

MR. BRELAND: Yes, Sir.

MR. SMITH: Your Honor, we think this is highly incompetent, this whole part of the case. And as far as the pictures being introduced here, nothing has been shown as to the way they were taken or the manner in which they were taken, and nothing of that kind has been shown or provided. No one has testified to the competency of the photographs. And we say that they are highly incompetent.

THE COURT: With reference to that, I believe the witness testified that the pictures taken—that one of them is a picture of her son that was taken shortly after Christmas, and I believe the witness testified that it is a true likeness of her son during his lifetime.

And she also testified that the picture taken in Chicago after his death portrays a true picture of what she saw there at that time.

Now, the Court is going to admit these pictures and evidence—that is, one picture there that she produced, so that the jury may see the likeness of Emmett Till during his lifetime.

And the Court is going to let be introduced into evidence the picture made in Chicago after his death. It will be cut from the paper, and the paper itself will not be any part of the exhibit.

And another thing, there will be no reference to any newspapers to which this witness may subscribe in Chicago, or any reference to what she may read. And there will be no reference or anything said about any newspapers or pictures other than this picture which she has identified as being a picture of her son taken after his death as she saw it there in Chicago. That picture will be permitted.

And there will be no reference to any other pictures or newspapers, or any reference as to what this witness may have read or subscribed to whatsoever. These pictures that the Court is permitting to be introduced into evidence are for the benefit of the jury, so that they may see a likeness of Emmett Till during his lifetime, and also a likeness of his body, as the witness stated, as she saw it in Chicago after the body was returned to Chicago.

MR. BRELAND: There is one other thing, Your Honor, that I think we ought to go into before the jury returns, and I think possibly there might be some objection to it.

THE COURT: Well, whatever you have for this witness of that nature, then let's get it out while the jury is still out.

MR. BRELAND: All right, Sir.

Q: Mamie, you said that you discussed your son's trip down to Mississippi several times with him before he left your home in Chicago, is that correct?

A: Yes, Sir.

Q: Did you caution him how to conduct himself and behave himself while he was down here in Mississippi before he left there?

A: Yes, Sir.

Q: Now, you have quoted in the press—I don't know whether you said it or not, but the press report shows it in quotation that you are supposed to have made, in these words, now listen carefully, and it says: "I told him several times before he left for Mississippi that he should kneel in the street and beg forgiveness if he ever insulted a white man or white woman." Now, did you tell him that?

A: Not those exact words.

Q: Well, what did you tell him?

A: I will give you a liberal description of what I told him. I told him when he was coming down here that he will have to adapt himself to a new way of life. And I told him to be very careful about how he spoke and to whom he spoke, and to always remember to say "Yes, Sir" and "No, Ma'am" at all times.

And I told him that if ever an incident should arise where there would be any trouble of any kind with white people, then if it got to a point where he even had to get down on his knees before them, well, I told him not to hesitate to do so. Like, if he bumped into somebody on the street, well, and then they might get belligerent or something, well, I told him to go ahead and humble himself so as not to get into any trouble of any kind. And I told him to be very careful how he walked in the streets at all times.

Q: And did you direct his attention as to how to act around white people, and how to conduct himself about a white man? The paper says that you cautioned him about his behavior before any white men. Did you call his attention to that?

A: Yes, Sir.

Q: And did you specifically indicate to him and caution him not to do anything to any white man so as not to bring on any trouble?

A: Yes, Sir.

Q: And from the newspaper quotation, the newspaper report says that you did that several times, is that true?

A: I did. I impressed it on him very carefully as to how he should act while he was down here.

Q: He had been in Mississippi before, had he?

A: Yes, Sir.

Q: And he had visited here close to Sumner before?

A: Yes, Sir, with that same uncle.

Q: And that was after he got to be a big boy, was it?

A: I think he was about nine years old then.

Q: And those are the only two times that he has been in Mississippi, so far as you know?

A: No, Sir. He came down here once when an infant, about 15 months old, maybe something like that. I know he was a small baby.

And then I think he came down here again while he was very small, maybe four or five years old. And then he was down here when he was about nine, and then this last trip.

Q: And did you caution him in those conversations you had with him not to insult any white women?

A: I didn't specifically say white women. But I said about the white people. And I cautioned him not to get in a fight with any white boys. And I told him that, because, naturally living in Chicago, he wouldn't know just how to act maybe.

Q: Prior to his coming down to Mississippi, and prior to his leaving Chicago, while he was living there in Chicago, had he been doing anything to cause you to give him that special instruction?

A: No, Sir. Emmett has never been in any trouble at any time.

Q: And he has never been in a reform school?

A: No, Sir.

Q: And he never had any trouble in any way with any white people?

A: No, Sir.

Q: I believe you live on the south side in Chicago, is that right?

A: Yes, Sir, on the south side.

Q: And that is the part of Chicago referred to as the black belt, is that right?

A: Yes, Sir.

Q: And the people in the community, are they all colored people or white people?

A: There are a few white people living there.

Q: And they have their homes there, is that right?

A: Yes, Sir.

THE COURT: Now is that all?

MR. BRELAND: Yes, Sir.

THE COURT: Now, the objections to all that testimony will be sustained, and there will be no questions along that line whatsoever. And since the Court has ruled on the pictures, the objection to all the testimony is sustained. And there will be no further reference to it, and there will be no questions asked concerning that after the jury comes in.

(The jury returned to the courtroom, and the proceedings continued with the jury present.)

Q: This,THE COURT: I think all that was in, Mr. Breland, before the jury retired. But you may proceed with the examination.

Q: And your son did leave your home in Chicago with the expectation of coming to Mississippi, is that right?

A: Yes, Sir.

Q: And you didn't come with him?

A: No, Sir.

Q: Now, I hand you what purports to be a photograph of your son. Is that a photograph of your son?

A: Yes, Sir.

Q: And that is a true and correct photograph of your son at the time it was taken?

A: Yes, Sir.

Q: And when was that picture taken?

A: This was made in my home two days after Christmas of 1954.

Q: Right after Christmas of 1954?

A: Yes, Sir. It was on about the 27th of December.

MR. BRELAND: We now ask that this photograph be identified which has already been marked as Exhibit 1 to the testimony of this witness for the purpose of identification.

Q: Now I will hand you what purports to be another photograph. Will you look at it and tell the court and jury what this is?

A: This is a picture of my son after he was sent back to Chicago dead. This is the way I saw him the second time. He had his clothes put on his body then. When I saw him the first time, he didn't have any clothes.

Q: And how much time elapsed from the time you first saw him without clothes until you saw him in the likeness of that photograph there?

A: I saw the one with his clothes on and without the clothes on the same day. Perhaps a half an hour or an hour had elapsed. I am not clear on that.

Q: And was the first view you had of your son there before the clothes were put on the body a likeness of the photograph shown here? That is, was it like the picture shown in that photograph?

A: The face, Yes, Sir.

Q: And everything was the same except that clothes had been put on the body the second time you saw him, is that right? That is, it was the same as it was when you saw him the first time when he had no clothes on, is that right?

A: No, Sir. The first time I saw him, he had a hole in his head up here (indicating with her hand), and that was open. And he had another scar. I can't tell you exactly where it was. It was either over the right eye or the left eye. I can't remember just now.

And he had a gash in his jaw, and his mouth was open and the tongue was out. That is the first time when I saw him without his clothes on. But from this picture here, it seems like his mouth has been closed, and that gash was sewn up, and that place in his forehead up there has been closed up. That is the way it looks to me.

Q: Then the photograph there is a better picture of him than the way it was when you first saw him, is that right?

A: Yes, Sir.

MR. BRELAND: This is the photograph that we asked to be marked as Exhibit to the testimony of this witness for the purposes of identification. You may take the witness.

MR. SMITH: That is all, if the Court please.

(WITNESS EXCUSED)

DOCUMENT 12: EMMETT TILL MURDER TRIAL TRANSCRIPT, DIRECT EXAMINATION OF CAROLYN BRYANT

CAROLYN BRYANT TESTIMONY, *STATE OF MISSISSIPPI VS. J. W. MILAM AND ROY BRYANT*, IN THE CIRCUIT COURT SECOND DISTRICT OF TALLAHATCHIE COUNTY, SEVENTEENTH JUDICIAL DISTRICT, STATE OF MISSISSIPPI, SEPTEMBER TERM, 1955, 261–280.

CAROLYN BRYANT

A witness introduced for and on behalf of the State, being first duly sworn, upon her oath testified as follows:

DIRECT EXAMINATION

By Mr. Carlton[5]:

Q: What is your name, please, ma'am?

A: Mrs. Roy Bryant.

Q: You are the wife of one of the defendants in this case the defendant Roy Bryant, is that right?

---

5   Sidney Carlton was one of the five local defense attorneys that represented Roy Bryant and J. W. Milam.

A: Yes, Sir.

Q: How old are you, Mrs. Bryant?

A: Twenty-one.

Q: And how tall are you?

A: Five feet, two inches.

Q: How much do you weigh, Mrs. Bryant?

A: One hundred and three pounds.

Q: Do you have any children?

A: Yes.

Q: What are those children's names?

A: Roy Bryant, Jr., and Thomas Lamar Bryant.

Q: And they are both boys, I believe?

A: Yes.

Q: What is Roy Jr.'s age?

A: He is three.

Q   And how old is Thomas Lamar?

A: Two.

Q: How old is your husband, Mrs. Bryant?

A: Twenty-four.

Q: When were you all married?

A: April 25, 1951.

Q: Did Roy serve in the Armed Forces?

A: Yes.

Q: When did he enlist in the Armed Forces?

MR. SMITH: We object, Your Honor. That is incompetent, immaterial, and irrelevant.

THE COURT: The objection is overruled.

Q: When did he enlist in the Armed Forces?

A: In June of 1950.

Q: That was about ten months, I believe, before you married?

A: Yes.

Q: How long did he stay in the service?

A: Three years.

Q: Did he get out in about June of 1953 then?

A: Yes.

Q: Now Mrs. Bryant, I direct your attention to Wednesday night, on the 24th of August, on that evening, who was in the store with you?

MR SMITH: If the Court please, we object to anything that happened on Wednesday evening unless it is connected up.

MR. BRELAND: We will connect it.

THE COURT: Will the jury please retire to the jury room.[6]

(The jury retired to the jury room, and the proceedings continued in the absence of the jury.)

Q: Mrs. Bryant, on Wednesday evening or Wednesday night, the 24th day of August, 1955, did anyone—who was in the store with you that night?[7]

A: No one.

Q: You were alone in the store at the time?

A: Yes.

Q: Was there anyone in the living quarters at the rear of the store?

A: Yes.

Q: Who was back there?

A: Mrs. Milam and her two children and also our two children.

Q: Did any incident occur in that store on that evening which made an impression on you?

A: Yes.

Q: And what time of the evening was that?

A: About eight o'clock.

Q: Was that before or after dark?

A: After dark.

Q: Just tell the Court what happened there at that time, please, ma'am.

A: This ni**er man came in the store and he stopped there at the candy case.

Q: And in the store, where is the candy case located?

A: At the front of the store.

---

6 After the jury left the courtroom, prosecution and defense lawyers presented opposing views regarding whether Carolyn Bryant should be allowed to testify about Emmett Till's visit to Bryant's Grocery and Meat Market. After a lengthy discussion, the presiding judge sided with the defense team's perspective and granted them the opportunity to question Carolyn Bryant about her interactions with Till during his visit to the store. The lengthy discussion has been omitted for the sake of brevity and clarity.

7 The jury remained out of the courtroom during the defense team's examination of Carolyn Bryant.

Q: And on which side is it?

A: It is on the left side as you go in.

Q: And that is the first counter there, is that right?

A: Yes, Sir.

Q: Now, is [sic] the store, with reference to that candy counter, is there anything back of the candy counter towards the wall of the store?

A: No.

Q: Is there any place to walk there or anything of that sort?

A: Yes, an aisle.

Q: When this negro man came in the store, where were you in the store?

A: I was farther back in the store, behind the counter.

Q: Where were you in the store when this man came in?

A: I was farther back behind the counter.

Q: Were you on the same side or on the other side?

A: The same side.

Q: And when he came in, I believe you said he stopped in front of the candy counter, is that right?

A: Yes.

Q: And what did you do then?

A: I walked up to the candy counter.

Q: And what transpired up there at the candy counter?

A: I asked him what he wanted.

Q: And did he tell you?

A: Yes.

Q: Do you know what it was he asked for?

A: No.

Q: And did you then get the merchandise for him?

A: Yes. I got it and put it on the top of the candy case.

Q: And what did you do then?

A: I held my hand out for his money.

Q: Which hand did you hold out?

A: My right hand.

Q: Will you show the Court how you held your hand out?

A: I held out my hand like this (demonstrating by holding out her hand.)

Q: Which hand was that?

A: My right hand.

Q: And will you show the Court how you did that?

A: Like this (demonstrating by holding out her hand).

Q: And did he give you the money?

A: No.

Q: What did he do?

A: He caught my hand.

Q: Will you show the Court just how he grasped your hand?

A: Like this (demonstrating with her hand).

Q: By what you have shown us, he held your hand by grasping all the fingers in the palm of his hand, is that it?

A: Yes.

Q: And was that a strong grip or a light grip he had when he held your hand?

A: A strong grip.

Q: And will you show the Court what you did? How did you get loose?

A: Well, I just jerked it loose, like this (demonstrating).

Q: It was about that difficult to get loose, was it?

A: Yes.

Q: And it was with that much difficulty that you got your hand loose?

A: Yes.

Q: Just what did he say when he grabbed your hand?

A: He said, "How about a date, baby?"

Q: When you freed yourself, what happened then?

A: I turned around and started back to the back of the store.

Q: You did what?

A: I turned to get to the back of the store.

Q: Did you do anything further then?

A: Yes. He came on down that way and he caught me at the cash register.

Q: You say he caught you?

A: Yes.

Q: How did he catch you?

A: Well, he put his left hand on my waist, and he put his other hand over on the other side.

Q: How were you going down along the counter there? Did he approach you from the front, or from the rear or how?

A: From the side.

Q: Now, Mrs. Bryant, will you stand up and put my hands just where he grasped you? Will you show the Court and jury?

A: It was like this (demonstrating by putting Mr. Carlton's hands on her body).

Q: He grabbed you like that, did he?

A: Yes.

Q: In other words, with his left arm around your back?

A: Yes.

Q: And his left hand on your left hip?

A: Yes.

Q: And he had his right hand on your right hip?

A: Yes.

Q: Did he say anything to you then at the time he grabbed you there by the cash register?

A: Yes.

Q: What did he say?

A: He said, "What's the matter, baby? Can't you take it?"

Q: He said, "What's the matter, baby? Can't you take it?"

A: Yes.

Q: Did you then try to free yourself? Was it difficult? Did you succeed in freeing yourself?

A: Yes.

Q: Did he say anything further to you at that time?

A: Yes.

Q: What did he say?

A: He said, "You needn't be afraid of me."

Q: And did he then use language that you don't use?

A: Yes.

Q: Can you tell the Court just what that word begins with, what letter it begins with?

A: (The witness did not answer verbally, but shook her head negatively.)

Q: In other words, it is an unprintable word?

A: Yes.

Q: Did he say anything after that one unprintable word?

A: Yes.

Q: And what was that?

A: Well, he said—well— "with white women before."

Q: When you were able to free yourself from him, what did you do then?

A: Then this other ni**er came in the store and got him by the arm.

Q: And what happened then?

A: And then he told him to come on and let's go.

Q: Did he leave the store willingly or unwillingly?

A: Unwillingly.

Q: How did the other negro get out of the store then? How did they leave?

A: He led him by the arm and led him out.

Q: Were there any white men in the store at the time this occurred?

A: No.

Q: Were there any other negro men in the store at the time?

A: No.

Q: Were there any other persons outside the store?

A: Yes.

Q: Were they white men or colored men?

A: Colored.

Q: Were there a number of them out there? How many of them were out there?

A: Oh, about eight or nine.

Q: When he went out the door, did he say anything further after he had made these obscene remarks?

A: Yes. He turned around and said, "Good-by."

Q: And when he got out the door, what did you do?

A: I called Mrs. Milam to watch me and then I ran out the door to go to the car.

Q: Which car did you go to?

A: Mrs. Milam's.

Q: What did you go to the car for?

A: For my pistol.

Q: Where was your pistol in the car?

A: Under the seat.

Q: It was under which seat?

A: The driver's seat.

Q: As you went out the door and went to the car, did you see this man again?

A: Yes.

Q: Where was he then? Where was he standing?

A: He was standing by one of the posts on the front porch.

Q: Your store has a front porch to it?

A: Yes.

Q: And these posts are on the front porch?

A: Yes.

Q: Did he say or do anything at that time?

A: He whistled and then came out in the road.

Q: Can you give a sound something like the whistle that he made there? Was it something like this? (Mr. Carlton demonstrated by giving two low whistles.)

A: Yes.

Q: When you got your pistol, Mrs. Bryant, where was this boy then? Or I should say where was this man?

A: When I turned around, he was getting in a car down the road.

Q: Did you rush back in the store then?

A: Yes.

Q: Had you ever seen that man before?

A: No.

Q: Have you ever seen him since?

A: No.

Q: Tell us what size man he was. Describe about how tall he was.

A: He was about five feet, six inches tall.

Q: And that is about four inches taller than you are, is that right?

A: Yes.

Q: And how much would you say that we weighed?

A: Around one hundred and fifty pounds.

Q: Did he walk with any defect?

A: No.

Q: Did he have any speech defect?

A: No.

Q: Did you have any trouble understanding him?

A: No.

Q: What sort of impression did this occurrence make on you?

A: I was just scared to death.

Q: Mrs. Bryant, do you generally know the negroes in that community around Money?

A: Yes.

Q: What kind of store is it that you run there?

A: It is just a general store.

Q: Are most of your customers negroes or white people?

A: Most of them are negroes.

Q: And of course, you come in contact with most of the negroes around there in that way?

A: Yes.

Q: And you know most of them around there, do you?

A: Yes.

Q: And was this man one of those?

A: No.

Q: Did he talk with a southern or northern brogue?

A: The northern brogue.

Q: Did you have any difficulty understanding him?

A: No.

Q: Did you have any white men anywhere around there to protect you that night?

A: No.

Q: Was your husband out of town?

A: Yes.

Q: Do you know where he was?

A: He was in Brownsville.

Q: What was his purpose in being away from home then?

A: He had carried a load of shrimp there.

Q: Where had he started out with that load of shrimp?

A: From New Orleans.

Q: When did you expect him home?

A: I didn't know.

Q: What was the reason for Mrs. Milam and the children being there with you?

A: So that I wouldn't be alone.

MR. CARLTON: Now, we submit, Your Honor, that the testimony here is competent on the basis of the testimony which was introduced by the State to show that there was some talk in Money, and to remove the minds of the jury the impression that nothing but talk had occurred there.

THE COURT: The Court has already ruled, and it is the opinion of the Court that this evidence is not admissible.

(The jury returned to the courtroom, and the proceedings continued with the jury present.)

MR. CARLTON: We have no further questions, Your Honor.

MR CHATHAM: No questions.

(WITNESS EXCUSED.)

DOCUMENT 13: FAIR TRIAL WAS CREDIT TO MISSISSIPPI

GREENWOOD MORNING STAR, SEPTEMBER 23, 1955

Those who were expecting anything but a fair and impartial trial, in which both the State and Defense did their best to product the facts in evidence, were disappointed with the manner in which the Milam-Bryant case was handled.

James L. Kilgallen, dean of American crime reporters[,] told *The Morning Star* editor yesterday for the second time that Miss. had certainly conducted the whole affair in a way which reflects only credit upon the state. He said, "I have never seen any people who have gone out of their way to see that this trial has been given both sides in this case. I have enjoyed my visit here in Miss. immensely, and hope to be able to come back again and again on more pleasant matters."

This was one of those cases where the radicals and NAACP sympathizers were hoping that Miss. would give them occasion to lambaste our state because of its being a segregation stronghold. They were alert to every possibility and played every angle. Sometimes they wore your patience thin, but Miss. people rose to the occasion and proved to the world that this is a place where justice in the courts is given to all races, religions, and classes.

The top newsmen at the trial were unanimous in their opinions that the trial was fair and impartial. Your editor talked to men whom all three press service, the United Press, the Associated Press and the international News[,] had covering the trial and they were agreed on this point.

Miss. has been raised in the opinion of many who are in position to be competent critics in this matter of justice.

DOCUMENT 14: TILL'S MOM, DIGGS BOTH DISAPPOINTED

MATTIE SMITH COLIN, *CHICAGO DEFENDER*, OCTOBER 1, 1955

Both Mrs. Bradley, mother of the slain Emmett Till, and Rep. Charles C. Diggs, an observer at the proceedings in Sumner, expressed disappointment in the outcome of the trial upon their arrival in Chicago last week.

During a brief stop-over enroute to Detroit, Diggs said, "I am disappointed. I went to Sumner with the hope that the Till trial would result in a conviction."

When asked if he planned to propose any legislation as a result of what he observed at the trial, the Congressmen replied: "I have some legislation in already to give the Justice Department the right to intervene in Civil Rights Cases and from this new experience I hope to strengthen our case for legislation that would have more than the presently casual regard for Negroes trying to participate in the elections."

He continued: "I am interested in something that would assure the right to vote to all citizens. The bias of the selection of the jury is the voter and the public officials are elected by the voters. An anti-lynch bill and legislation to eliminate the poll tax are the basic solutions I believe for this. I still have hope that the people will wake up to the international significance of this."

Diggs spoke in Detroit Sunday, at a meeting sponsored by the NAACP.

He said he did not know at this point whether he would observe the trial for the kidnapping charges against Roy Bryant and J. W. Milam, to be held in Leflore County sometime in November.

Mrs. Bradley shared the spotlight with A. Philip Randolph of the Brotherhood of Sleeping Car Porters rally Sunday in New York City. Commenting on the Mississippi trial she remarked: "It's about the biggest farce I have ever seen. It is unbelievable and fantastic."

She added: "I do not feel that there will be a conviction on the kidnapping charge in view of the arguments raised at the murder trial."

Hysterical and in tears, Mrs. Alberta Spearman, grandmother of Emmett, shook her head and said: "I am not quick to make comments but I think it was unfair and I feel beyond a doubt that they are guilty."

She said she was prepared for the possibility of an acquittal before the hearing was over and had decided to leave as soon as the jury retired.

To her surprise a reporter asked her, before the hearing ended, what she intended to do after the acquittal, which Mrs. Bradley said gave her the impression "that it was sewed up from the day it started."

Mrs. Bradley with disgust in her voice told of how the "friendly" whites entered the courtroom each morning and greeted her, Congressman Diggs and the Negro press with, "Good morning N . . ." and the unfriendly whites just glared . . . and questioned the legality of a Negro congressman . . .

Bishop Louis H. Ford, who delivered the eulogy at the funeral of young Till, in commenting on the "not guilty" verdict said: "It hurts, but it is good, maybe the Congress of the United States will do something about this, and it points out to the nation the evils of Mississippi."

DOCUMENT 15: EXCERPT FROM "THE SHOCKING STORY OF AN APPROVED KILLING IN MISSISSIPPI"

WILLIAM BRADFORD HUIE, *LOOK* MAGAZINE, JANUARY 24, 1956

Had there been any doubt as to the identity of the "Chicago boy who done the talkin'," Milam and Bryant would have stopped at the store for Carolyn to identify him. But there had been no denial. So they didn't stop at the store. At Money, they crossed the Tallahatchie River and drove west.

Their intention was to "just whip him . . . and scare some sense into him." And for this chore, Big Milam knew "the scariest place in the Delta." He had come upon it last year hunting wild geese. Over close to Rosedale, the Big River bends around under a bluff. "Brother, she's a 100-foot sheer drop, and she's a 100 feet deep after you hit."

Big Milam's idea was to stand him up there on that bluff, "whip" him with the .45, and then shine the light on down there toward that water and make him think you're gonna knock him in.

"Brother, if that won't scare the Chicago ——, hell won't."

Searching for this bluff, they drove close to 75 miles. Through Shellmound, Schlater, Doddsville, Ruleville, Cleveland, to the intersection south of Rosedale. There they turned south on Mississippi No. 1, toward the entrance to Beulah Lake. They tried several dirt and gravel roads, drove along the levee. Finally, they gave up: in the darkness, Big Milam couldn't find his bluff.

They drove back to Milam's house at Glendora, and by now it was 5 a.m. They had been driving *nearly three hours*, with Milam and Bryant in the cab and Bobo lying in the back.

At some point when the truck slowed down, why hadn't Bobo jumped and run? He wasn't tied; nobody was holding him. A partial answer is that those Chevrolet pickups have a wraparound rear window the size of a windshield. Bryant could watch him. But the real answer is the remarkable part of the story.

Bobo wasn't afraid of them! He was as tough as they were. He didn't think they had the guts to kill him.

Milam: "We were never able to scare him. They had just filled him so full of that poison he was hopeless."

Back of Milam's home is a tool house, with two rooms each about 12 feet square. They took him in there and began "whipping" him, first Milam, then Bryant smashing him across the head with those .45s. Pistol-whipping: a court-martial offense in the Army . . . but MP's have been known to do it . . . and Milam got information out of German prisoners this way.

But under these blows Bobo never hollered—and he kept making the perfect speeches to ensure martyrdom.

Bobo: "You bastards, I'm not afraid of you. I'm as good as you are. I've 'had' white women. My grandmother was a white woman."

Milam: "Well, what else could we do? He was hopeless. I'm no bully; I never hurt a ni**er in my life. I like ni**ers—in their place—I know how to work 'em. But I just decided it was time a few people got put on notice. As long as I live and can do anything about it, ni**ers gonna stay in their place. Ni**ers ain't gonna vote where I live. If they did, they'd control the government. They ain't gonna go to school with my kids. And when a ni**er even gets close to mentioning sex with a white woman, he's tired o' livin.' I'm likely to kill him. Me and my folks fought for this country, and we've got some rights. I stood there in that shed and listened to that ni**er throw that poison at me, and I just made up my mind. 'Chicago boy,' I said, 'I'm tired of 'em sending your kind down here to stir up trouble. Goddam you, I'm going to make an example of you—just so everybody can know how me and my folks stand.'"

So Big Milam decided to act. He needed a weight. He tried to think of where he could get an anvil. Then he remembered a gin which had installed new equipment. He had seen two men lifting a discarded fan, a metal fan three feet high and circular, used in ginning cotton.

Bobo wasn't bleeding much. Pistol-whipping bruises more than it cuts. They ordered him back in the truck and headed west again. They passed through Doddsville, went to the Progressive Ginning Company. This gin is 3.4 miles east of Boyle: Boyle is two miles south of Cleveland. The road to this gin turns left off U.S. 61, after you cross the bayou bridge south of Boyle.

Milam: "When we got to that gin, it was daylight, and I was worried for the first time. Somebody might see us and accuse us of stealing the fan."

Bryant and Big Milam stood aside while Bobo loaded the fan. Weight: 74 pounds. The youth still thought they were bluffing.

They drove back to Glendora, then north toward Swan Lake and crossed the "new bridge" over the Tallahatchie. At the east of this bridge, they turned right, along a dirt road which parallels the river. After about two miles, they crossed the property of L. W. Boyce, passing near his house.

About 1.5 miles southeast of the Boyce home is a lonely spot where Big Milam has hunted squirrels. The river bank is steep. The truck stopped 30 yards from the water.

Big Milam ordered Bobo to pick up the fan.

He staggered under its weight . . . carried it to the river bank. They stood silently . . . just hating one another.

Milam: "Take off your clothes."

Slowly, Bobo sat down, pulled off his shoes, his socks. He stood up, unbuttoned his shirt, dropped his pants, his shorts.

He stood there naked.

It was Sunday morning, a little before 7.

Milam: "You still as good as I am?"

Bobo: "Yeah."

Milam: "You've still 'had' white women?"

Bobo: "Yeah."

That big .45 jumped in Big Milam's hand. The youth turned to catch that big, expanding bullet at his right ear. He dropped.

They barb-wired the gin fan to his neck, rolled him into 20 feet of water.

For three hours that morning, there was a fire in Big Milam's back yard: Bobo's crepe-soled shoes were hard to burn.

Seventy-two hours later—eight miles downstream—boys were fishing. They saw feet sticking out of the water. Bobo.

The majority—by no means *all*, but the *majority*—of the white people in Mississippi 1) either approve of Big Milam's action or else 2) they don't disapprove enough to risk giving their "enemies" the satisfaction of a conviction.

DOCUMENT 16: MAMIE BRADLEY'S UNTOLD STORY (INSTALLMENT VIII)

MRS. MAMIE BRADLEY, *CHICAGO DEFENDER*, JUNE 9, 1956

While I was lying there, wide awake, I pondered over the whole chain of events leading up to that fateful day. My mind went back and forth over my life like a roving camera searching, searching, for some reason why this had happened to me. I was angry with God that He had let Bo be kidnapped and slain so brutally and aloud I demanded, "Why did You do this? Why are You so cruel that You would let this happen? Why do You allow this kind of persecution?"

STRANGE EXPERIENCE

Then began one of the strangest experiences of my whole life. It was just as though someone had entered the room and we were carrying on a conservation. It was as real to me as though we were both flesh and blood.

The presence said to me, "Mamie, it was ordained from the beginning of time that Emmett Louis Till would die a violent death. You should be grateful to be the mother of a boy who died blameless like Christ. Bo Till will never be forgotten. There is a job for you to do now."

I sat up in bed and stretched out my hand. I was praying hard that nobody would come up front before the conversation was completed, because I wanted the answer and I wanted to finish talking this thing out.

I knew that if anyone came up there and heard me talking, they would instantly think I had gone out of my mind with grief.

VOICE GIVES ANSWER

"What shall I do?" I asked.

The voice replied, "Have courage and faith that in the end there will be redemption for the sufferings of your people and you are the instrument of this purpose. Work unceasingly to tell the story so that the truth will arouse men's consciences and right can at last prevail."

The voice died away and the Presence left the room. I lay down and slept peacefully.

There is no need to go into all of the details of the killing and the funeral. I have read the magazine article purporting to be the real story of the Till Killing.

Roy Bryant and J. W. Milam went to great pains to manufacture those lies about Bo in order to try and justify the crime they committed.

NO REST, NO PEACE

What they said is the true reflection of the warped and twisted minds of people like them. They are insane with hatred and that hate comes from fear and insecurity bred into them.

In their brazen admission of the killing, they have condemned themselves forever along with the state of Mississippi.

There will never be any rest or peace for them.

I could hate all white people for this, but I don't.

I think, however, that the large class of decent people in this country are guilty of the sins of omission when they fail to speak out for the right and take a stand against injustice. These are the people I am appealing to.

That's why I am telling the story of my life and Bo's.

He was a child, sweet and innocent. Nothing can change that. I sit and I think. I have time for a lot of thinking.

BO'S RESPONSIBILITY

I think back now about the elderly woman living on an old age pension by herself and how fond Bo was of her. He used to go by her house every day to see if she was all right and to run errands for her and he would never take any money from her. She was his special responsibility.

I think of Bo imitating the commercial announcers on TV and how funny he could be.

I think of our discussions and plans for his college education—and how that would lead into the inevitable thought that some day he would get married and have children of his own.

I used to get jealous at the thought of one day having a daughter-in-law and I would even fuss with Bo about her.

BO'S FUTURE

He used to laugh so hard at me. He'd say, "You know what? I'm going to get a great big house to keep you both in and when you get to quarreling, I'll just pick you both up—one in each hand and I won't let you go until you both promise to be good."

Sometimes, I'd find myself actually pouting about Bo's future wife.

Then I had a dream. I saw a baby—the most beautiful child I had ever seen. It was Bo's baby and I fell in love with it.

When I woke up, I could still imagine myself holding this child—my grandchild and the thought made me feel all warm and good. After that, I found myself eagerly looking forward to Bo's marrying and having children. They would be my grandchildren.

WHAT IS LEFT

I am alone now. I have my mother and father, my relatives and friends. Still I am alone with my thoughts and my heart buried in a pine box underneath glass.

I haven't started back to work yet, because I have not yet become adjusted to being without Bo.

There is work for me to do and I am thinking of the future. I may go back to school and prepare myself to teach.

At 33, I should have some useful years ahead and I think I would enjoy working with children.

The doctors tell me that I could marry again and have children. This, I don't know about. Right now, I'm alone with Bo and God.

PART IV
CONCLUSION

FURTHER READING

Blue, Bonnie. *Emmett Till's Secret Witness: FBI Confidential Source Speaks*. Park Forest, IL: BL Richey Publishing, 2013.

DeLuca, Christine Harold, and Kevin Michael. "Behold the Corpse: Violent Images and the Case of Emmett Till." *Rhetoric and Public Affairs* 8, no. 2 (2005): 263–286.

Gorn, Elliot J. *Let the People See: The Story of Emmett Till*. New York: Oxford University Press, 2018.

Houck, Davis W. "From Money to Montgomery: Emmett Till, Rosa Parks, and the Freedom Movement, 1955–2005." *Rhetoric and Public Affairs* 8, no. 2 (2005): 175–176.

———. "Killing Emmett." *Rhetoric and Public Affairs* 8, no. 2 (2005): 225–262.

Houck, Davis W., and Matthew A. Grindy. *Emmett Till and the Mississippi Press*. Jackson: University of Mississippi Press, 2010.

Hudson-Weems, Clenora. *Emmett Till: Sacrificial Lamb of the Civil Rights Movement*. Bloomington, IN: AuthorHouse, 2006.

———. "Resurrecting Emmett Till: The Catalyst of the Modern Civil Rights Movement." *Journal of Black Studies* 29, no. 2 (1998): 179–188.

Kolin, Phillip C., Aaron Kramer, and Clyde R. Appleton. "Forgotten Manuscripts: 'Blues for Emmett Till': The Earliest Extant Song about the Murder of Emmett Till." *African American Review* 42, no. 3–4 (2008): 455–460.

Mace, Darryl. *In Remembrance of Emmett Till: Regional and Media Responses to the Black Freedom Struggle*. Lexington: University of Kentucky Press, 2014.

Mark, Rebecca. "Mourning Emmett: 'One Long Expansive Moment'." *Southern Literary Journal* 40, no. 2 (2008): 121–137.

Metress, Christopher. "Langston Hughes's 'Mississippi-1955': A Note on Revisions and an Appeal for Reconsideration." *African American Review* 37, no. 1 (2003): 139–148.

———. "'No Justice, No Peace': The Figure of Emmett Till in African American Literature." *MELUS* 28, no. 1 (2003): 87–103.

———. *The Lynching of Emmett Till: A Documentary Narrative*. Charlottesville: University of Virginia Press, 2002.

Nelson, Marilyn. *A Wreath of Emmett Till*. Boston: Graphia, 2009.

Peterson, James Braxton. "The Revenge of Emmett Till: Impudent Aesthetics and the Swagger Narratives of Hip-Hop Culture." *African American Review* 45, no. 4 (2012): 617–631.

Priest, Myisha. "The Nightmare is Not Cured: Emmett Till and American Healing." *American Quarterly* 62, no. 1 (2010): 1–24.

Russell, Margaret M. "Reopening the Emmett Till Case: Lessons and Challenges for Critical Race Prejudice." *Fordham Law Review* 73 (2005): 2101–2132.

Schwabauer, Barbara A. "The Emmett Till Unsolved Civil Rights Crime Act: The Cold Case of Racism in the Criminal Justice System." *Ohio State Law Journal* 71, no. 3 (2010): 653–698.

Smith, Valerie. "Emmett Till's Ring." *Women's Studies Quarterly* 36, no. 1–2 (2008): 151–161.

Tell, Dave. *Remembering Emmett Till*. Chicago: University of Chicago Press, 2019.

Tisdale, John R. "Different Assignments, Different Perspectives: How Reporters Reconstruct the Emmett Till Civil Rights Murder Trial." *Oral History Review* 29, no. 1 (2002): 39–58.

Tyson, Timothy. *The Blood of Emmett Till*. New York: Simon and Schuster, 2017.

Wideman, John Edgar. "The Louis Till Blues Project." *Callaloo* 34, no. 1 (2011): 1–17.

———. *Writing to Save a Life: The Louis Till File*. New York: Scribner, 2016.

QUESTIONS FOR DISCUSSION AND FURTHER RESEARCH

The following questions are crafted in such a way to spark deeper engagement with the graphic history and the primary sources contained within the volume. The central theme is how the Emmett Till murder engendered competing narratives and had differing ramifications over time.

1. Why was Till's youth and presumed innocence such an important part of how the murder case was reported in black newspapers? Why does it matter that he was innocent and perhaps naive about Southern racism and violence?

2. How might Till's murder been viewed had he been eighteen or older? Do you think the response to his murder would have been similar or different?

3. J. W. Milam, Roy Bryant, and Tallahatchie County authorities conspired to keep Till's body out of public view. What did they hope to accomplish in doing so? If they had succeeded, how might the absence of visual imagery have impacted public interest and perceptions of the case?

4. Photographs of Till's body lying in his casket made his murder a topic of national and international conversation. How and why did these photographs matter?

5. Within the context of white Mississippi newspaper reporting, how did the narrative regarding the Till case seemingly shift over time, and how did the shift(s) potentially matter to the outcome of the trial?

6. In the context of newspapers owned and operated by blacks, such as the *Chicago Defender*, how was Till portrayed? What does this portrayal tell us about the politics of race and identity in America?

7. During Carolyn Bryant's trial testimony, how did she portray Till? What did the prosecution seek to accomplish through portraying him in this way? More broadly, what was the purpose of Carolyn Bryant's testimony?

8. What are the differences between Mamie Till's portrayal of Emmett Till and Carolyn Bryant's portrayal? How might Mamie Till's portrayal of her son have shaped public opinion?

9. What are the implications of reframing the Till murder case as a conspiracy involving multiple people versus J. W. Milam and Roy Bryant as the lone perpetrators?

10. According to William Bradford Huie's "The Shocking Story of An Approved Killing," Milam and Bryant murdered Till because he was not afraid of them and he believed he was better than they were. Despite Milam and Bryant's self-serving explanation for murdering Till, they nonetheless portray him as an active agent rather than as a passive victim of Southern racial violence as many news reports suggested. What are the pros and cons of understanding Till as a historical agent?

11. Given that J. W. Milam, Roy Bryant, and other possible conspirators are either elderly or deceased, what is the benefit of recent FBI investigations into Till's murder?

12. Ultimately, was Till's murder trial a miscarriage of justice? Why or why not? If it was a miscarriage of justice, what can be done today to gain a measure of justice for Till and his family?

13. Why does Till's story continue to resonate in modern times? Why does he remain an important symbol? To whom does he matter?

14. What is the significance of Till's murder today?

THE EMMETT TILL MURDER: A TIMELINE

The 1955 murder of Emmett Till was a seminal event of the 1950s and it has continued to reverberate in contemporary American society. This timeline attempts to capture the most significant developments related to the case.

1955

Saturday, August 20, 1955—Accompanied by Mose Wright and Wheeler Parker, Emmett Till arrives in Money, Mississippi, to visit relatives.

Wednesday, August 24, 1955—Till and several cousins go to get candy at Bryant's Grocery and Meat Market in Money. During the visit, Till whistles at Carolyn Bryant.

Sunday, August 28, 1955—Roy Bryant and J. W. Milam kidnap Till from Wright's home in Money. Wright alerts the sheriff that Till has been kidnapped. Bryant is questioned by police, admits to having taken Till, and is arrested.

Monday, August 29, 1955—Milam confesses to having taken Till and is arrested.

Wednesday, August 31, 1955—Till's corpse is found floating in the Tallahatchie River. The body is prepared for burial in Mississippi but ultimately is shipped to Chicago.

September 2–6, 1955—Till's corpse arrives in Chicago. The public is able to view Till's brutalized body at Roberts Temple Church of God in Christ. Bryant and Milam are indicted for Till's kidnapping and murder.

September 19–23, 1955—Bryant and Milam stand trial for Till's murder and are found not guilty.

November 1955—The Leflore County grand jury decides not to indict Bryant and Milam for kidnapping Till.

1956

January 1956—*Look* magazine publishes an article by William Bradford Huie, "The Shocking Story of An Approved Murder," in which Bryant and Milam admit to having murdered Till.

2000

2003

January 2003—Mamie Till dies.

2004

February 2004—In a historic decision, the Federal Bureau of Investigation (FBI) announces it will reopen the Till murder case nearly fifty years after the original verdict.

2005

June 2005—Till's body is exhumed and DNA analysis confirms that it is Till's body.

2006

March 2006—The FBI releases an 8,000-page investigative report on the murder. Although heavily redacted, the report identifies multiple possible accomplices (some of whom were alive at the time) in the murder.

2007

February 2007—The Leflore County grand jury opts not to indict Carolyn Bryant and other possible co-conspirators in the Till murder.

2008

September 2008—Congress passes the Emmett Till Unsolved Civil Rights Crime Act.

LYNCHING AND RACIAL VIOLENCE IN AMERICAN HISTORY: A TIMELINE

The story of Emmett Till is intimately connected to the history of segregation, disenfranchisement, and racial violence in America society. This timeline highlights key events that are germane to the broader historical context.

1868

1868—The first Ku Klux Klan organization is founded in Pulaski, Tennessee.

1875–1876—Through violence, intimidation, and voter fraud, white Democrats overthrow Reconstruction-era governments in Mississippi and South Carolina.

1890—The Mississippi state constitution disenfranchises black voters. Other Southern states follow suit over the next decade.

1892—Ida B. Wells publishes *Southern Horrors*, a pamphlet that details the lynching of black Americans. More documented lynchings of black Americans occur in 1892 than any other year.

1896—The *Plessy v. Ferguson* Supreme Court decision approves separate but equal public accommodations, which paves the way for *de jure* segregation in the South.

1900

1900—Robert Charles is lynched in New Orleans; Ida B. Wells publishes *Mob Rule in New Orleans* in protest.

1901—W. E. B. Du Bois publishes his classic text *The Souls of Black Folk*, which frames what it means to be black in American society.

1908—The Springfield race massacre erupts and the National Association for the Advancement of Colored People (NAACP) is founded.

1911—Laura Nelson and her teenaged son, L. D. Nelson, are lynched in Okemah, Oklahoma.

1915—D. W. Griffith's film *The Birth of a Nation* is released, and the second iteration of the Ku Klux Klan organization is established.

1916—Black youth Jesse Washington is lynched in Waco, Texas.

1919

1919—Widespread racial violence against black Americans, commonly referred to as the "Red Summer," engulfs American cities.

1921—The Tulsa race massacre, among the deadliest race massacres in American history, occurs in Tulsa, Oklahoma.

1922–1930s—The NAACP petitions Congress to pass federal antilynching legislation.

1931—The Scottsboro Nine are charged and imprisoned for allegedly raping two white women in Alabama.

1938—Richard Wright publishes the novella *Uncle Tom's Children*, which features stories of lynching and white terrorist violence.

1941—World War II commences in Europe.

1942—Japanese internment begins.

1943—Wartime anti-black violence enflames Detroit and Harlem.

1951—*We Charge Genocide: The Crime of Government Against the Negro People* is published.

1955—Emmett Till is murdered in Mississippi. The Montgomery bus boycott begins in Montgomery, Alabama.

1958—Civil rights activist Clara Luper and the local NAACP Youth Council begin a six-year-long sit-in movement in downtown Oklahoma City, Oklahoma. Due to their efforts nearly every white-owned downtown business is desegregated by the passage of the Civil Rights Act of 1964.

1959—Black power activist Robert F. Williams publishes a self-defense manifesto, *Negroes with Guns*.

1963—Civil rights activist Medgar Evers is murdered in Mississippi, and the 16th Street Baptist Church bombing in Birmingham, Alabama, makes manifest the massive white resistance to the civil rights movement.

1964—Civil rights activists James Chaney, Andrew Goodman, and Michael Schwerner are murdered in Mississippi as they attempt to register black voters. The Civil Rights Act of 1964 becomes law.

1965—During the "Bloody Sunday" protests, Dr. Martin Luther King, Jr., and other black marchers are attacked by Alabama state troopers at the Edmund Pettus Bridge. The Voting Rights Act of 1965 goes into effect.

1967—Poverty and alienation spark black urban rebellions during the "Long Hot Summer."

1968—Dr. Martin Luther King, Jr., and Fred Hampton, chairman of the Illinois chapter of the Chicago Black Panther Party for Self Defense, are assassinated.

USING EMMETT TILL: A GRAPHIC HISTORY IN THE CLASSROOM

Meaningful learning in the classroom can only take place when a culture of inclusivity and mutual respect between the instructor and student is established. Teaching difficult histories of race and racial violence—more so than other aspects of American history—creates complicated classroom dynamics for instructors and students alike. These classroom dynamics can pose challenges to nurturing an inclusive classroom environment. Specifically, classroom texts and discussions that utilize or reference racial epithets can undermine an instructor's best efforts to create an inclusive classroom culture if not approached with sensitivity and empathy.

This graphic history contains allusions to the "n" word, violent scenes, and references to lynching. I do not shy away from these difficult topics in this book because they reflect the everyday, historically accurate, racial realities of the Jim Crow South; and therefore, they are indispensable to creating a realistic portrayal of the Emmett Till murder. Confronting racial realities, which includes racially derogatory language, is pedagogically important, however, it is also important that instructors confront racial realities within the classroom with sound pedagogical strategies.

To this end, recommendations for teaching and discussing The Murder of Emmett Till in the classroom follow. These recommendations will emphasize classroom transparency, contracting with students, and inclusive discussion strategies. This guidance is not exhaustive and is to be understood as an entry point for how to create a classroom environment that is conducive for engaging a text that represents a difficult history, infused with racially derogatory content. Trust building and permission granting are on-going relational activities; they are not singular events that occur only at the beginning of the semester or at the front end of a particular text.

TRANSPARENCY

Transparency is critical for building trust in the classroom and it is important for gaining student assent to engage with difficult histories. The syllabus for a course in which this graphic history is assigned should explain that the course will analyze and discuss difficult histories that contain racial epithets. Most importantly, the syllabus should clearly explain the learning goals for using texts such as this one. Instructors should revisit these course goals in transparent, dialogic conversations with their students before beginning this text. Students need to engage in conversation about the pros and cons of using a text that contains racial epithets.

CONTRACTING

Contracting creates clear expectations and ground rules with students for grappling with difficult histories and ones that include racial epithets. Students and instructors work together to discuss how members of the discussion will engage with the text and engage with each other so that all members of the classroom feel heard and respected. Contracting establishes specific classroom behaviors and norms that guide how discussion moves forward and how it can be redirected or stopped if necessary. This contractual agreement should be clearly outlined before the first discussion and it should be revisited with reflections and with room for revisions. Contracting does not have to be a lengthy list of rules. At its root, contracting is about trust. Listening, shared ownership, personal responsibility and other aspects of healthy classroom norms can all be boiled down to creating trust in the classroom community.

By having discussions about and gaining consensus on how to approach difficult histories in the classroom, the instructor and students build trust together and co-create expectations for the course. Some key questions to discuss/gain consensus on are listed below:

- Are students/the instructor allowed to say aloud/directly reference racially derogatory language (in reference to the text or otherwise) in the classroom? Why or Why not?

- If not, will euphemisms/symbolic language such as the "n-word" be used as substitutes for directly referencing racially derogatory language? Why or why not?

- If a conversation involving racially sensitive content becomes uncomfortable or offensive, will there be "safe words" (previously negotiated and recognized by students) that indicate that the discussion needs to be halted until questions/concerns are addressed?

- Are students permitted to exit (and return to) class if they need time to collect themselves and process racially sensitive/offensive content?

INCLUSIVE DISCUSSION STRATEGIES

Establishing clear parameters for engaging in discussion is important to create inclusive discussions in relation to racially sensitive content. A discussion strategy that I have utilized in my classroom is to allow underrepresented students as well as those who are least comfortable/prepared to discuss difficult histories to speak first. (Students can be asked to journal or prepare thoughts ahead of class.) Organizing the conversation in this way allows underrepresented perspectives to frame the conversation. More broadly, it allows the parameters for engaging racially sensitive content to evolve (beyond what is outlined in the syllabus) in relation to student concerns and feedback. In my courses, this is the primary way through which I gain student assent and agreement for my approach to co-creating a shared space in which we can confront difficult histories in the classroom together.

SELECT BIBLIOGRAPHY

Please see the following resources for greater context and tools for engaging difficult histories involving race, racial violence, and racial epithets. My recommendations are not comprehensive; again, this list is a starting point:

Facing History and Ourselves. "Discussing Sensitive Topics in the Classroom." https://www.facinghistory.org/mockingbird/discussing-sensitive-topics-classroom.

Randall Kennedy. *Nigger: The Strange Career of a Troublesome Word*. New York: Vintage, 2003.

Michelle Kenney. "Teaching the N-Word." Rethinking History. https://www.rethinkingschools.org/articles/teaching-the-n-word.

Elizabeth Stordeur Pryor. "The N-Word in the Classroom." Tedx Easthampton Women. https://www.ted.com/talks/the_n_word_in_the_classroom/up-next.

Public Broadcasting Service. "N Word." https://www.pbs.org/wgbh/cultureshock/teachers/huck/section1_2.html.